Life After Death
A Widow's Story

Life After Death
A Widow's Story

A Shattered Life Put Back Together

Nina W. Cooper

Life After Death A Widow's Story A Shattered Life Put Back Together

Published by Nina Will Publishing
Division of Nina Will LLC
743 Elm St.
Flossmoor, IL 60422
708-772-1716
ninawillllc@outlook.com

ISBN: Paperback 979-8-9879652-1-4
Library of Congress Control Number: 2023905798

Cover Design by Taylor Owens

Edited by Denise K. Gates

Photograph by Karen Forsythe Photography, Homewood, IL

In Memory of My Beloved

His love was better than wine.
My lord sat at his table.
My spikenard sent forth his fragrance.
A bundle of myrrh
was my well-beloved unto me.
My beloved was mine and I was his;
His desire was toward me.
He ravished my heart with just one glance.
He was love, joy, peace, longsuffering, gentle,
good, meek, and temperate.
He was faithful to the call
of the Lord to come home.
He was my Song of Solomon.
Paul described his "fruit of the Spirit" attributes
in Galatians 5,
and Jesus spoke of him in Luke 15.
I called to him, but he gave me no answer;
I sought him, but I could not find him.
He was whisked away by our Lord.
Beloved, I will see you again,
and I rejoice with you now
and will rejoice with you again
at His banquet table!

All my Love, Nina.

"The Spirit itself bears witness with our spirit, that we are the children of God: and if children, then heirs; heirs of God, and joint-heirs with Christ; if so be that we suffer with Him, that we may be also glorified together. For I reckon that the sufferings of this present time are not worthy to be compared with the glory which shall be revealed in us. For the earnest expectation of the creature waits for the manifestation of the sons of God. For the creature was made subject to vanity, not willingly, but by reason of Him who has subjected the same in hope, because the creature itself also shall be delivered from the bondage of corruption into the glorious liberty of the children of God. For we know that the whole creation groans and travails in pain together now. And not only they, but ourselves also, which have the firstfruits of the Spirit, even we ourselves groan within ourselves, waiting for the adoption, . . .the redemption of our body. For we are saved by hope:

but hope that is seen is not hope:
for what a man sees, why does he
yet hope for? But if we hope for
that we see not, then do we with
patience wait for it"
(Romans 8:16-25).

Table of Contents

Introduction...1

Chapter 1 4
    My Beloved

Chapter 2.. 15
    The Event

Chapter 3.. 32
    In the Beginning

Chapter 4.. 42
    Grief Encounter

Chapter 5.. 54
    Offense

Chapter 6.. 66
    Joy Stealers and Widow Killers

Chapter 7.. 75
    Encourage Yourself and Praise the Lord

Chapter 8.. 83
    I Visited Him in Heaven

Chapter 9.. 91
    Lust of the Flesh

Chapter 10.. 96
    The Journey Continued

Chapter 11.. 109
    Anybody for Me?

Chapter 12 .... *113*
   Reminiscing-A Reliable Reminder of Trust

Chapter 13 .... *134*
   Battle Royal

Chapter 14 .... *148*
   A Supposed Easy Prey

Chapter 15 .... *161*
   The Depths of Love

Chapter 16 .... *174*
   Regrets

Chapter 17 .... *183*
   Tried by Fire Refined into Gold

Chapter 18 .... *195*
   Epilogue-Victorious Ending

Introduction

I made it through the wilderness of grief. As I traveled through mourning, God humbled me; and as I longed for release from my pain, He fed me with manna that I did not know and that I had not eaten before. He gave me the sustenance I needed in a depth that I had not experienced before. The manifestation of characteristics of God occurred in my life as I surrendered to Him as my burden bearer, comforter, peace-giver, provider, a shoulder to cry on, and a lap to sit in.

Consumed by grief my Lord satisfied my appetite of all that I desired and hungered for, freedom from torment. He made me to know that I lived not by bread alone but by His Word. He clothed me with a garment that did not wear out. I adorned the garment of praise instead of a spirit of heaviness. My feet did not swell nor did my shoes wear out as I walked through the journey of sorrow over the departure of my husband. God shod my feet with His peace.

Throughout my lamentation, God chastened me as any parent would chasten their child and encouraged me to keep His commandments, walk in His ways, and fear Him. God kept His promise and brought me into the good land of the living that flowed with the abundance of waters of wellness and good things to eat where I lacked nothing. I broke through anguish that had me bound.

I received and basked in His blessings on the other side—in the promised land of contentment in Him with a shattered life put back together. He lifted up my heart and placed me in a beautiful dwelling place void of grief. God brought me out of the parched place of anguish where fiery serpents and scorpions tried to destroy my faith and God allowed the tempter to bite and sting. But by the power of His Holy Spirit, I did not perish in the desert of pain or succumb to my enemy's will but remained in the will of my Lord and His good pleasure for my life (Deuteronomy 8; Isaiah 61:3; Philippians 2:13).

"The Lord is nigh unto all them that call upon Him, to all that call upon Him in truth. He will fulfil the desire of them that fear Him:

He also will hear their cry, and will save them" (Psalm 145:18-19).

Chapter 1

My Beloved

On December 27, 2017, my husband Ron left this world. When I spoke of his departure, I hesitated to say that I lost him because "lost" also implied something that could be found. Though I expected to see my beloved again, I felt it inappropriate to say that I would find him or that he would be returned unto me. My faith, hope, and trust in the Lord gave me confidence that we would see and know one another again. Even though we would be no longer married to one another (Luke 20:34-36), I knew that we—together along with others—would experience a new and different kind of love.

I held on to the promise that in the new heaven and earth marriage is only to the Lamb of God (Revelation 19:7). However, in life on the present earth, my husband and I were one flesh (Genesis 2:24); and separation from part of me initiated a deluge of anguish and a sense of incompleteness. I clung to the truth that all I needed to fill the emptiness left behind abided in me, and I escaped the void Ron's departure left in my mind, body, soul, and spirit. I learned my only recourse: Trust in what Jesus proclaimed. He and the Holy Spirit dwelled in me and would bring me comfort.

"And I will pray the Father, and He shall give you another Comforter, that He may abide with you for ever; even the Spirit of Truth; whom the world cannot receive, because it sees Him not, neither knows Him: but you know Him; for He dwells with you, and shall be in you. I will not leave you comfortless: I will come to you"
(John 14:16-18).

To obtain relief from grief, I purposed to tap into the power and love within me and in which I inhabited. I am in Christ, He is in me, and together we resided in the Father—the God of Abraham, Isaac, and Jacob. Throughout my journey, with frequency I reminded myself of this intrinsicality that personified me.

"At that day you shall know that I am in My Father, and you in Me, and I in you. He that has My commandments, and keeps them, he it is that loves Me: and he that loves Me shall be loved of My Father, and I will love him, and will manifest Myself to him" (John 14:20-21).

The Holy Spirit reminded me that God created me in Christ Jesus (Ephesians 2:10). I depended upon and reached for the love of the Father and His Son.

"Jesus answered and said unto him, If a man love Me, he will keep My words: and My Father will love him, and We will come unto him, and make Our abode with him" (John 14:23).

The Lord walked me through endurance and encouraged my demonstration of faith as I experienced grief. With trepidation, I thrust myself into the presence of the Lord. My gut wrenched, and I shook as I sobbed and pleaded with God to mend my shattered life, remove the heaviness of mourning, and give me peace. My inner battle was to live a life of faith from a position of repose as I moved closer towards perfection every step of the way. I contended to enter into His rest and stay there. From that position of tranquility in Christ, I received the promise: The Kingdom of God within me on earth as ordained in heaven—the Lord's will for my life (Matthew 6:10; Luke 17:21). Thus, I attained relief from my pain.

"Come unto Me all you that labor and are heavy laden, and I will give you rest. Take My yoke upon you, and learn of Me; for I am meek and lowly in heart: and you shall find rest unto your souls. For My yoke is easy, and My burden is light"
(Matthew 11:28-30).

"You will keep him in perfect peace, whose mind is stayed on You: because he trusts in You"
(Isaiah 26:3).

Many questioned the status of my beloved's salvation. Because he was known as an atheist, a practitioner of some New Age activities, and a follower of objectivism, they doubted that he now lived in Christ. My husband had proclaimed the death of God. But I surmised that he had believed at one time that God lived. Ron knew the Word. Once, I quoted a biblical truth to him, and he responded with the book and verse scripture reference. On more than one occasion when we were out of the country and faced adversity, he encouraged my acts of prayer.

I knew, though, that knowledge of the Word did not represent belief. What was evidence of the power of God to me, for the most part, symbolized foolishness to him (1 Corinthians 1:18). Ron justified his opinion of a deceased God through juxtaposition in a supposed being who was supreme over all with the question, "How could there be a God when there is so much injustice, suffering, pain, and poverty in the world?" He admitted that in the past he had felt a few goose bumps but maintained that he had never encountered nor experienced manifestations of Christ, God the Father, or the Holy Spirit. He said that he had not seen any burning bush (Exodus 3:2). Because he had not seen or heard, he could not believe in the unseen or unheard God. He also could not accept the absolute truth of the Word. Existence on the earth included injustice (Matthew 5:44-45), suffering (2 Corinthians 1:3-6), pain (Revelation 21:4), and poverty (Matthew 26:11).

Yet, at Ron's last hour, on his bed in the emergency room with me and our son (legally his stepson, but my son has corrected me and says, "That is my Dad") while he breathed, spirit still in body, Chris prompted his father several times to accept Christ. And Chris discerned that Ron did accept and confess Jesus as his Lord before he left and his flesh died.

How Ron's life ended brought me contentment. However, I still faced a quagmire. Though I longed to be with my husband asleep in Christ (2 Corinthians 5:6-8; 1 Thessalonians 4:13-18), and no longer live as a stranger on the earth (Psalm 119:19), I knew I had to continue on without my beloved. My heart was, is, and will always be heaven bound, one who groans within myself along with all of creation waiting for my adoption, a manifest son of God, conformed to the image of Christ (Romans 8:16-23; 28-29; Ephesians 1:3-6). But still Ron's departure brought me torment. My beloved left me behind to continue my journey on earth without him and accomplish the Father's will for my life.

I have replied to those who questioned Ron's salvation with my belief that the Lord Jesus Christ not only saved me but also my household (Acts 16:31). Long ago, my husband heard the Word of truth and believed it. At the moment my beloved accepted truth the Holy Spirit sealed the promise—his redemption (Ephesians 1:13-14). God foreknew my husband; and even though Ron had strayed for a season, by the power of the Holy Spirit, death could not separate him from the love of God in Jesus (Romans 8:29, 38-39). My beloved conquered death in his final moments on earth through his reactivation of faith (John 5:24).

Nevertheless, some retorted, "Did he confess it with his mouth?" When I stated my assurance of my husband's salvation because the Word said it and the Lord confirmed it, they sent a look of pity and doubt my way. Pity because they thought my spouse's condemned soul instigated languishment. Doubt because they disbelieved my affirmations. Well, I ended the conversation and let them wallow in their own faithlessness, religiosity, and fear because they could not imagine salvation attained outside of their mindset. They did not realize that the devil used them as a pawn to instill fear, steal and kill joy, and promote the agenda of the anti-Christ spirit. They did not walk in love at that moment but hate and despised the sight of me that reflected the light of Christ. Only satan would take advantage of a widow's vulnerability and tell her that he had her husband with intent to torment her, sift her like wheat, and instill fear and doubt.

Even a pastor had "lovingly" commented (indirectly to me as he talked to someone else, but so I could hear), "Everybody thinks their loved one is saved." In this statement, void of love and full of craftiness, I discerned the influence and characteristic of my adversary (Ephesians 4:11-16). God has proclaimed that He gave saints the honor to execute the judgment written (Psalm 149:6-9). I knew that the enemy had, in that moment, deceived the mouth that spoke. Together, they had concluded that they had the authority to write, knew what God wrote, could judge what the Lord wrote, or had been granted sight to see the names written in the Book of Life—and that my beloved's name was excluded (Revelation 20:15). In a few moments of time, their mouths uttered lies for this pronouncement of judgment by man did not affirm God's proclamation. But as Jesus similarly told Peter, I said to myself and in silence directed the thought towards that person, "Get thee behind me, satan; you are an offense to me. You know nothing of the plans of God and speak lies" (Matthew 16:23; John 8:44).

The devil who hated me and the light within me exploited man to taunt, laugh at, and scorn me. The spirit behind that mouth bit and tried to devour (Galatians 5:15). Hate in them came out—works of the flesh, instead of the fruit of the Spirit. God confirmed the truth to me about where my beloved dwelled on more than one occasion, and the enemy still made its attempts to cause me to doubt God's Word.

The Holy Spirit exemplified the opposite. He fulfilled the promises of God and was my Comforter, forever in me—my teacher of all things and reminder of what the Lord spoke (John 14:16-17; 26). Throughout my ordeal, I thanked God for His Spirit that endued me with power to move through my day, gave me assurance of His presence, bestowed upon me peace, and encouraged my heart not to be troubled (John 14:27). My Lord and Savior prayed for me and strengthened me so that my faith did not fail me.

> *"And the Lord said, Simon, Simon, behold, satan has desired to have you, that he may sift you as wheat: But I have prayed for you, that your faith fail not: and when you are converted, strengthen your brethren" (Luke 22:31-32).*

From this stance and trust, I lived, reminded myself, and voiced to God and all of the heavens and earth exactly what belonged to me. I moved myself to be in alignment with my Lord's promises. I understood that the devil did only what my Father allowed. And what God permitted served to strengthen and test me and to show satan faith in operation on earth. My Father ensured that when Jesus returned He would find faith in me (Luke 18:8).

> *"I am the Lord, and there is none*

else, there is no God beside Me: I
girded you, though you have not
known Me: that they may know
from the rising of the sun, and from
the west, that there is none beside
Me. I am the Lord, and there is
none else. I form the light, and
create darkness: I make peace, and
create evil: I the Lord do all these
things" (Isaiah 45:5-7).

I was reborn spiritually 14 months after my beloved and I married; and for 21 years, I prayed and battled for my husband's rebirth. I experienced metamorphosis in December 1996; and 21 years later in December so, too, did my Ron.

Chapter 2

The Event

Ron started his journey on December 26 and left in the early morning of the 27th. Unbeknownst to me, God had put into motion five days earlier Ron's final days on earth before He whisked him away home.

On the 21st, he asked if I considered that we were like the show, *Designated Survivor*.[1] We had enjoyed this political drama until illness superseded his desire or ability to engage with television. I asked, "In what way?" And he responded, "How the president had to protect and work for the nation." The Spirit in me stirred, and in quietness I questioned, "How could we accomplish that? And what would you do?" He replied, "I don't know, but I will do the best that I can." And he implied that

---

[1] From Wikipedia, the free encyclopedia: *Designated Survivor* is an American political thriller drama television series created by David Guggenheim originally released 9/21/2016 – 6/7/2019.

the assignment of designated survivor belonged to me.

Dumfounded, I went upstairs and mulled over our conversation. I summarized what I heard the Spirit say through my husband: "Do not have any pity party or dillydally. Get on with life. Get on with the fight for this nation." My husband did not know my recent prayers or the revelation that because Abraham, my father, did not withhold his only son all the nations of the earth would be blessed in his seed and that covenant included me, the seed of Abraham (Genesis 22:15-18; Galatians 3:7, 26-29). The Holy Spirit brought to my remembrance my assignment from the Lord to demonstrate that blessing through prayer not only for America but also for the many nations He put on my heart to pray that they would not be turned into hell but saved (Psalm 9:17; Revelation 21:24).

I was reminded of Ezekiel's call to be a watchman for the house of Israel and through prophetic acts how he portrayed the iniquity of Israel and Judah, and God's judgment (Ezekiel 2:1-3:11, 3:16-7:27). I knew God called me to be an intercessor for nations to cry out for repentance, forgiveness of sins and God's mercy but in caring for my husband I had neglected His mandate.

> *"If I shut up heaven that there be no rain, or if I command the locusts to devour the land, or if I send pestilence among My people; If My people, which are called by My Name, shall humble themselves, and pray, and seek My face, and turn from their wicked ways; then will I hear from heaven, and will forgive their sin, and will heal their land"* (2 Chronicles 7:13-14).

My mind flooded with thoughts, and I wept. God used my husband to remind me not only to continue to pray for our nation, but for all the nations, people, and groups listed on my prayer wall. Ron had inferred my designated survivor's position, and that I should get on with the battle for nations through prayer. There was no time for commiseration. He believed disease would destroy his life, and I had to continue without him. I had received a reminder of my commission, release, and orders from my beloved. I do not know if he realized or understood that God implemented him as His instrument. But that exemplified God's character. God utilized whomever and whatever He chose. Employed by God, Ron spoke volumes to me.

I went back downstairs, took his hand, and told Ron I loved him. I expressed sorrow for any hurt I had caused or disappointments he experienced with our marriage. My heart filled with compassion, and it grieved me to witness the deterioration of his body. I did not want him to be in pain; I wanted him to have peace. I thought and felt as if I was releasing Ron to go, and he had prepared me for his departure. Also earlier in the month, prompted by the Holy Spirit, I focused on being subject unto my husband in all things (Ephesians 5:22-24). In that tender moment, I submitted myself to my husband—including the release he desired. I let go and let my husband's will rule. My beloved knew and accepted the journey before him. He told me that I did not concede to the progression of his disease and diagnosis. In that, we were in agreement. In my heart, I always hoped and believed that Ron would be healed. I had not let go.

But my resolve did not last. I went back a few minutes later and told Ron that "we" were designated survivors. That political drama represented a fictional series of events; our lives and situation were a real story. A man of few words, Ron waved me away and disregarded my attempt to reopen the conversation. Perhaps frustrated, he may have tired of my continued push to sustain his life. I withdrew so he would have peace.

Questions though raged through my mind. I wondered if Ron would see tomorrow or be here for Christmas. He loved the Christmas season. In anguish, I mulled. I did not wish for him to endure more; yet, at the same time, I held out for my beloved to be made whole. In conclusion, I refused to put a sentence of limited longevity on Ron just as I had refused to place him under hospice care. I accepted no man's timetable for his departure, including my husband's. I surmised that only God knew when my beloved's life would end on the earth.

The next day, December 22, Ron ate one good meal—his last supper. He also asked about the date. He never had inquired about a period of time before. I believe Ron knew death knocked at his door. Perhaps he waited for what he foreknew would be his last day on earth. I have asked myself, "Did ministering spirits from God visit and foretell Ron his final day?" It reminded me of my mom. During her last days, she watched the clock and pointed to it with a peaceful expectancy as if she waited for a particular time. I think she also knew. With my dad, my mother said he had asked a few days before he went home, what choir came by and sang in his room. My mother had gently replied that no choir had visited him, but she pondered what he said.

I did what I had to do on a daily basis until God did what I knew He could do. I expected the Trinity[2] to move—to cause heaven and earth to shake and virtue to

---

[2] From Wikipedia, the free encyclopedia: The Christian doctrine of the Trinity is the central doctrine concerning the nature of God in most Christian churches, which defines one God existing in three coequal, coeternal, consubstantial divine persons: God the Father, God the Son (Jesus Christ) and God the Holy Spirit, three distinct persons sharing one homoousion (essence); "each is God, complete and whole." See also 1 John 5:7.

flow from Jesus into my beloved's mind, body, spirit, and soul.

I had become a strong and lean 5-foot 9-inch, 140-pound woman dead weight-lifting a 130-pound man. As his mobility decreased, I had ordered belts and equipment, watched videos, and received advice from his therapist on how to move and lift him without injury to myself. Nevertheless, one time I had to convince him to view a video with me on how I could get him off the floor after he slid off the couch. He did not want me to call the paramedics. We succeeded even though I flipped over the ottoman backwards. After he cried out to make sure I did not hurt myself, we laughed.

During the progression of his illness, I could sense the difficulty he experienced in acceptance of, resolve to need, and dependence upon my assistance. Be that as it may, the transformation of his surrender brought our marriage to a position of fullness that had not existed before. Still, I feared I would reinjure my lower back. I recognized my sensitivity due to previous car accidents and other stress inducers. Although I had conquered back discomfort with wisdom, exercise, and weight control, I experienced uneasiness that my body would fail and not endure. Nonetheless, I wanted to be the one to care for him—for no one else would do.

God entrusted my husband's care to me, and I purposed to continue no matter what. Yes, I could have prayed, "Lord, in Jesus' name, give me the strength to care for Ron" or declared, "I can do all things through Christ which strengthens me" (Philippians 4:13). Although the enemy taunted me that I would grow weary in my well doing (Galatians 6:9), I expected God to heal my husband despite doctors' prognosis and the degeneration of his body that occurred before my eyes.

On December 26th my beloved's last full day I saw Ron for the first time shed a tear and witness God's Spirit prepare him to come home. That morning I discovered that the night before had not gone well. The monitor did not pick up his moan for help, and I found his bell in his bed rather than on the hospital bed table. He had dropped the bell before he could ring it, and the covers muffled any sound.

I felt guilty when I found him wet, soiled, and cold. I asked myself, "Why didn't you come down and check on him?" When I awakened that morning, I realized that for the first time in months I had slept without interruption. I could not comprehend why the Holy Spirit or my spirit by instinct had not roused me. When I went to bed, I set up all he needed, but it did not remain so through the night. I tortured myself with the question, "Why didn't I wake up and perceive that Ron needed my help?"

Comprehension came later as I reminisced about his last day. The manifestation of the finished work of the cross would be realized in my husband during his final hours on earth. God gave me tranquility through a night's sleep to face a new chapter in the journey of faith. Each milestone I ventured ended in triumph because, as I grasped my Lord and did not let go, virtue flowed from Jesus to me and God's love and promises engulfed me every step of the way.

> *"Every word of God is pure: He is a shield unto them that put their trust in Him" (Proverbs 30:5).*

Later on that morning after I got my husband settled; the thought came to me to anoint my beloved with oil and pray over him. In the early afternoon, the Holy Spirit prompted again. I called Chris to come and join me. Although Ron waived me off as I started, Chris and I continued in prayer and my husband listened. I anointed my beloved with oil. A teardrop fell from his right eye. Never had I witnessed Ron shed a tear.

Later that evening I gave Ron his bath and dressed him in fresh disposable underwear, undershirt, and pajamas. I checked the bandage on the bedsore at the bottom of his tailbone. He agonized in pain as I moved him from side to side to put fresh linen on his bed for the night. No longer able to speak, he moaned. But, like his usual self, he did so subdued.

I knew that my husband preferred his head to be slightly elevated, so I indicated that I had to let his head down so that I could shift his body up nearer the top of the bed. My 6-foot 2-inch husband just fit his extra-long hospital bed, but only with his head at the top. He sighed in weariness. Movement caused discomfort. I got on the bed and straddled him. On my knees, I took hold of the edges of the waterproof pad and lifted and inched him up the bed. He grimaced. Now 130 pounds—down from a healthy 220—he could no longer help push his body up. As I indicated, "Just a little more, honey," and raised him again, I said to myself, "Lord, I do not know how much longer I can do this." The concern about my continued ability to endure veiled a cry from my heart: "God, it is time for you to shake, rattle, and roll—time to heal Ron, time to move." In less than three hours of my silent prayer, God did just that.

I accomplished my tasks, got Ron's covers settled on his bed, and made sure his feet had plenty of room at the bottom to move around. I pointed to the twin mattress, moved to the floor, and reminded him that I would sleep nearby to come to his aid as needed.

I kissed him and told him I would be right back after I changed into my night gown. He nodded. Upstairs, I washed my face, brushed my teeth, and put on my night gown and bathrobe. I wore my fleece bathrobe because on the floor it might be colder. I came downstairs and went over to the mantle and unplugged the Christmas lights on the garland strung around the fireplace and bookshelves. As I reached to turn off the floor lamp next to his bed, I told him, "Okay honey, goodnight; and remember I will be right over there," pointing to the mattress on the floor. I heard no response.

"Ron?" No response.

"Ron?" No response.

I went around to the other side of the bed and looked at his face. His eyes were open but there was no movement. I yelled, "Ron! Come back! Ron, come back!"

I heard Chris jump out of bed and run down the stairs. The paramedics came, and Ron was revived but was not conscious or in a communicative state. In his final moments in the early morning of the 27th upon his bed in the emergency room, he listened to encouragement from Chris. Our son discerned that his Dad, my beloved, accepted the salvation message.

Before Christ died, He proclaimed, "It is finished. Father, into your hands I commend my spirit," and He gave up His spirit (John 19:30; Luke 23:46). God shook the earth, rattled bones, caused the dead to arise out of graves, raised Christ from the dead, and sent an angel to roll back the stone of Jesus' tomb (Matthew 27:51-53; 28:2-6; Acts 2:22-24). I believe God did the same for my Ron, as He also did for my earthly father and mother. He shook heaven and earth, raised my husband up out of his grave of eternal death, rolled away all sin, shame, and guilt and made it no more, and sent an angel to escort him to his heavenly home (1 Corinthians 6:14).

When my husband's spirit left his body I know that the Father placed him in His Son's bosom. The reality, manifestation, and truth of the work of the cross from the foundation of the world occurred for, in, and through my beloved. Ron was raised up, placed in Christ and together they abided in the Father's bosom (Ephesians 2:4-7; John 1:18). I envisioned my beloved asleep in Christ, resting upon the bosom of Jesus in the Father and loved by both Father and Son (1 Thessalonians 4:13-14; John 14:19-21).

Afterwards, at home, I looked at his empty bed and thought of his body in the closed casket at the funeral home. A choice overcame me and a decision was placed before me: Ron with life in his earthly body or being present with the Lord. I knew that Christ could raise him to life. Ron's body was available and not embalmed because I knew that he would not want anyone to gaze at his frail body, which was a shadow of what they remembered. I had decided that it would be a closed-casket service and private with family and close friends only. Ron would not want strangers to walk by, gawk, and talk over or about him.

On the other hand, I corrected myself and thought that embalmment did not matter because even if I had it would not be a problem for Christ to raise him back to life on earth. Excitement filled me as I anticipated the sight of my beloved again. But then I paused and reflected, "How selfish of me." I asked myself, "If I was with Christ, would I want to come back?" and answered with assurance, "No!"

My husband had stopped the fight for his life. Yet I had not. I also questioned myself, "What if my perception of his resignation to death in actuality revealed his desire to go?" At that moment of contemplation, I released Ron and relinquished my own desire to see him returned to his body.

Later, though, at the funeral home as I gazed upon him one last time, in silent despair I uttered, "Jesus raise him." In my heart, I knew this would not be so. I had opted out of that choice. Anyway, I said to myself, "Who would want to come back to this world?" Nevertheless, I pondered why Ron left when I went upstairs and wondered "Why did he go before I came back?" We did not say goodbye. The same had happened with my mom. I left her room, and she departed. Man had put a death sentence on her also; still, I expected God to heal her. But God's will did not include restoration of health on earth for either of them.

I brushed the lint off Ron's suit jacket and made a mental note that they were not as meticulous with a closed casket. I remembered the surprised look on the staff's face when we came by to view the body. I reached and took the "Beloved Husband," "Beloved Father," and "Beloved Grandfather" medallions that were placed on the inside top of the casket. These I wanted with me to keep and give out accordingly. It blessed me to have Chris home for the holidays. It was perfect timing, as God knew what would take place, prepared beforehand, and arranged for our son to be with me. I praised the Lord who gave me strength as I maneuvered through final arrangements. Chris's steadfastness was my mainstay as he helped me through the initial stages of our bereavement, and we clung to and comforted one another.

After everything had been settled and Chris had returned to his out-of-state home, I walked into my empty home, left my boots at the door, and hung my coat in the closet. I put my hat, gloves, and scarf on the appropriate shelf and laid my car keys on the table in the foyer. This was my first night alone; in fact, it was the first time in my life that I lived by myself—no parents, siblings, husband, children, or pet. I also had no job because I had resigned to care for my husband.

As I sat at my dining room table in contemplation, I heard Ron's voice call me from downstairs—his weak and sickly voice that I had heard so many times. I jumped up and ran towards it, but I came to my senses at the top of the stairs, halted, and exclaimed, "No, you are not my husband; to be absent in the body is to be present with the Lord" (2 Corinthians 5:6-8). "Get out!"

I proceeded downstairs, went over to Ron's "bedroom" and declared again, "Whatever you are, you are not my husband." I never heard that voice again.

Chapter 3

In the Beginning

When we first learned of Ron's illness, he looked at me and said, "Aren't you supposed to lay hands on the sick and they recover?" (Mark 16:17-18). Hope and expectation filled his eyes and voice, but behind that was the spirit that mocked my faith and taunted me to assume a defensive position. Unbelief is evil (Hebrews 3:12). I refused to entertain or have any skepticism in my heart. The tempter failed in the attempt to mock God's Word. Satan succeeded with Eve in the garden (Genesis 3:1-6). But as he failed with Jesus, my role model, he did so also with me (Matthew 4:1-11; 1 John 3:2). The devil did not sway me. It was Jesus who healed, not me. Virtue had to flow from Christ to Ron (Luke 6:19).

I prayed for him to receive wholeness not only in silence when my hands were on him, but whenever I entreated the Lord. I petitioned for my husband to be delivered from the disease that clung to his body. I desired that Jesus would give me power as He gave His disciples to heal (Matthew 10:1). I wanted Ron freed from illness through my hands or words in the name of Jesus (John 14:13). Confident though in my prayers, I expected God to normalize his body by whatever means. I looked and waited for the reversal of his blood disease, myelodysplastic syndrome/myeloproliferative neoplasms.[3] Not alone in my prayers, others also pleaded to the Lord for his restoration.

I never saw myself being without Ron. I ignored the one-year lifespan prognosis with the likelihood of the progression of his disorder to blood cancer, leukemia. I did not believe in impossibility, only in the possibility of my beloved's release from the bondage of sickness (Mark 9:23). Too many times, the Lord had touched me. Too many times, He saved me from death. Too many times, He healed my body— even as He did with the woman with the

---

[3] National Cancer Institute, An Official Website of the United States Government, "Cancer Types, Myelo-proliferative Neoplasms," Patient Version: Myelodysplastic/myeloproliferative neoplasms are a group of diseases in which the bone marrow makes too many white blood cells. Myelodysplastic/myeloproliferative neoplasms are diseases of the blood and bone marrow.

issue of blood who reached out and touched Jesus and then her blood dried up (Mark 5:25-29). Although I was not plagued for 12 years, after the birth of my daughter I hemorrhaged profusely and received several pints of blood; however, I had continued to lose blood. When I was about to be taken for exploratory surgery, I cried out softly to myself two words, "No, God." I touched God's Son by faith and my blood flow stopped immediately.

I knew that Jesus did what the cross accomplished. The stripes He received removed infirmities from my body (Isaiah 53:5). Many times I cried out to Him, and He sent forth His Word and restored health to my body (Psalm 107:19-20). I have asked myself if I could have done something different for my Ron. My belief that Ron would be cured did not waiver when after a test analysis we were denied bone marrow transplant candidacy, which was one option the specialist gave in our initial consultation that had the possibility to prolong my beloved's life. The other option offered was chemotherapy, blood and platelet transfusions, and a plethora of drugs at various intervals. I stood firm with the expectation of Ron's blood cell production returning to normalcy. I never lost hope as my husband, medical practitioners, and I battled his disease through 43 pints of blood over 23 transfusions, 14 units of platelets by 14 platelet transfusions, 7 chemotherapy cycles of 12 days each, 5 hospital stays, weekly blood draws, and as required 14 prescription drugs, 4 over-the-counter medications, plus other drugs that were tried during hospitalizations.

Though his weekly blood count results fluctuated, I did not vacillate. My conviction in the manifestation of God's Word in my husband was assured. I requested that the Lord deliver Ron from the jaws of death, and by faith I believed it would be so. With patience, I waited on the Lord to return my beloved's health to wholeness as all of us involved participated in the fight against Ron's disease with the goal of sustaining his life. I did all I knew to do: Hold on to faith and love my husband.

"But let him ask in faith, nothing wavering. For he that wavers is like a wave of the sea driven with the wind and tossed. For let not

*that man think that he shall receive
any thing of the Lord. A double
minded man is unstable in all his
ways"* (James 1:6-8).

His nurse practitioner at the cancer center commented to me on more than one occasion, that she had seen a lot of couples and people but never observed anyone as dedicated as I was. I stood as a living testimony. My steadfastness through my beloved's illness served as an affirmation of faith in operation and example of the love and light of Christ. Others besides Ron's nurse practitioner also noticed. I received questions about my beliefs, and those who asked got answers and encouragement for their journey with God. In the midst of my husband's suffering, I still strengthened the brethren (Luke 22:31-32). The patients, their family members, and the healthcare workers that Ron and I encountered at the cancer center or hospitals noticed my convictions and were drawn to the love exhibited. They desired to comprehend and partake of what they saw demonstrated—some in the midst of their own despair, forlornness, and illness.

During one of my husband's chemo treatments, a man who also received chemotherapy, in frustration at not being able to get his feet raised in his chair, had more than once cried out in anguish, "I am dying here." The nurses had stepped away. I got up from the seat next to my husband, walked over, and adjusted the man's chair. Even before I approached, the Spirit of God went before me and calmed the man's spirit. God's love for him went ahead of me. The man's eyes expressed what he felt—gratitude for being loved and not being forsaken. As I interacted with others through our ordeal, I discerned that they wrestled with application of faith in their life. I perceived their hunger and hope for the same resolve they witnessed in me to manifest in their life. I received many "how" questions. I did what I thought every wife would do: That which God expected me to do. I performed as the counterpart of my husband, his helper.

> "And the Lord God said, 'It is not good that man should be alone; I will make him a helper comparable to him'" (Genesis 2:18, NKJV).

What Ron could not do for himself I did for him as I would with my own body. Ron and I walked and experienced his illness journey as one flesh.

"But from the beginning of the creation God made them male and female. For this cause shall a man leave his father and mother, and cleave to his wife; and they two shall be one flesh: so then they are no more two, but one flesh" (Mark 10:6-8).

Obedience to the declarations of God, a priority in my life, caused my love towards and for God to transcend my love for Ron. Though I loved my husband and loved mankind, first and foremost I strove to keep the commandments of God (1 John 5:1-3). Through my faith in God and His Son, Ron's disease did not rule us; but we overcame it, served as a living testimony, and saw victory in the end.

"For whatsoever is born of God overcomes the world: and this is the

victory that overcomes the world,
even our faith. Who is he that
overcomes the world, but he that
believes that Jesus is the Son of
God" (1 John 5:4-5)?

We denied death its sting and my beloved triumphed over cancer, assuming his heavenly position in Christ at the right hand of God. My husband completed his journey on earth and obtained that which God had ordained—God's gift by grace, salvation through faith.

"Behold, I show you a mystery; We
shall not all sleep, but we shall all
be changed, in a moment, in the
twinkling of an eye, at the last
trump: for the trumpet shall sound,
and the dead shall be raised
incorruptible, and we shall be
changed. For this corruptible must
put on incorruption, and this mortal
put on immortality. So when this
corruptible shall have put on
incorruption, and this mortal shall
have put on immortality, then shall
be brought to pass the saying that

is written, Death is swallowed up in victory. O death, where is your sting? O grave, where is your victory? The sting of death is sin; and the strength of sin is the law. But thanks be to God which gives us the victory through our Lord Jesus Christ"
(1 Corinthians 15:51-57).

"But God, who is rich in mercy, for His great love wherewith He loved us, even when we were dead in sins, has quickened us together with Christ, (by grace you are saved;) and has raised us up together, and made us sit together in heavenly places in Christ Jesus: that in the ages to come He might show the exceeding riches of His grace in His kindness toward us through Christ Jesus" (Ephesians 2:4-7).

On the last night we had together, I cupped Ron's face and his hands and asked him again to forgive me for not being a better wife or for anything I did. He nodded. I was not his Jesus, only his imperfect wife whom he left behind to work out her own salvation with fear and trembling (Philippians 2:12). During my husband's last days on earth, God—true to His character—gave me courage, strength, and wisdom to attend to my beloved's needs, be a light to the world, and positioned me to accomplish the next phase of my life (1 Chronicles 28:20; Proverbs 2:6; Philippians 2:14-16).

Chapter 4

Grief Encounter

*"For the Lord will not cast off for
ever: but though He cause grief, yet
will He have compassion according
to the multitude of His
mercies"* (Lamentations 3:31-32).

The enemy thought the departure of Ron
gave prime opportunity to annihilate my
hope for a promised future, derail my
destiny, drain life from me, and leave a
disintegrated shell of a human being. I was
confronted with separation from my
beloved and aloneness. God allowed the
tormentor to use my circumstance and
shroud me with a spirit of heaviness. His
tactics were to manipulate my bereavement
and make me succumb to anguish, fatigue,
and desolation.

Although God permitted satan's
harassment, my Lord accomplished His
intent. I experienced Christ and the power

of His resurrection in the midst of mourning. Grief, weakness, and isolation presented an opportunity for me to press toward my high calling of God of being conformed to the image of His Son as I journeyed through lamentation over my husband.

"Yes doubtless, and I count all things loss for the excellency of the knowledge of Christ Jesus my Lord: for whom I have suffered the loss of all things, and do count them but *dung, that I may win Christ, and be found in Him, not having mine own righteousness, which is of the law, but that which is through the faith of Christ, the righteousness which is of God by faith: that I may know Him, and the power of His resurrection, and the fellowship of His sufferings, being made conformable unto His death; If by any means I might attain unto the resurrection of the dead. Not as though I had already attained, either were already perfect: but I follow after, if that I may apprehend that for which also I am*

apprehended of Christ Jesus.
Brethren, I count not myself to
have apprehended: but this one thing
I do, forgetting those things which
are behind, and reaching forth unto
those things which are before, I
press toward the mark for the prize
of the high calling of God in Christ
Jesus" (Philippians 3:8-14).

Time and time again, the enemy tried to challenge my strength and my faith in the Lord and to place upon me a quarantine spirit that taunted me with thoughts that no one cared or understood. Though without companionship but never alone, I reached daily for Christ and the Holy Spirit in me to tap into their virtue and power and attain deliverance from my pain. In response to the devil's chasm, I clung to the truth of Christ in the Father, the Father in Christ, God in me, me in God, the Holy Spirit in me, I in Jesus, and Jesus in me (John 14:10; 1 John 4:15; Romans 8:9; 2 John 1:9).

With resolve, I affirmed the greatness of who I had in me over satan and his principalities (1 John 4:4). Although I was bombarded with agony, God gave me the ability to overcome their assault. I cried out to God and obtained relief as His Word lighted my path and His love encompassed me (Psalm 119:105; 5:12). I suited up every day for battle, trusted that the Lord would not turn me over to my oppressor, and kept my feet firmly planted in the way to my destiny as a joint-heir with Christ (Ephesians 6:10-11; Galatians 4:7). I did not have a failed expedition. Although I faltered at times, tossed about by waves of anguish, God never separated me from His love in Christ because of grief (Romans 8:35-39). Nothing could do that but me (2 Peter 1:1-11).

Bereavement became just another contention in my life that I overcame. I had both mountaintop and valley experiences where I gained a deeper understanding, knowledge, a demonstration of love by my Father, and increased my faith and trust in Him—but only as I yielded myself to His classroom. I willingly offered my complete self to His purpose for me. The Lord answered the tormented cry of my heart and met me with more of Him as I gave myself to Him. Many times, I succumbed to anguish and my flesh ruled. Nonetheless, all have sinned and come short of the glory of God, with me being no exception (Romans 3:21-26). I confessed my shortcoming, repented, picked myself up, turned back to my Lord, and moved on (1 John 1:8-10).

Nine days after my beloved's departure, I failed miserably. I experienced a day full of stress and did not handle it well. I missed my husband's presence and the division of household chores. He managed our finances. Though I paid the bills and we discussed money transactions, I never worried and trusted his advice and decisions. Nevertheless, I had to again take charge not only of my current financial picture but the management and completion of business transactions that came about with the death of a spouse. Ron also had handled all of the "technology" in our home. The Internet went down, and I lost it as I tried to get help from a live person with my provider. I even cursed. I asked myself, "Where did that profanity come from?" I surmised that what is in you comes out of you. "Well," I said, "the devil wants me to fail, but I will not give in or up."

I had started a fast a few days earlier and decided I would continue and just take communion. I pressed through with worship. I repented of my response to my frustrating day and asked for forgiveness. I longed for my husband but surrendered to God and knew He would see me through. I reminded myself that Christ saw me as His joy set before Him, a manifest son of God. I purposed to see myself as God did: Faith finished at His right hand.

> "Wherefore seeing we also are compassed about with so great a cloud of witnesses, let us lay aside every weight, and the sin which does so easily beset *us*, and let us run with patience the race that is set before us, looking unto Jesus the author and finisher of *our* faith; who for the joy that was set before Him endured the cross, despising the shame, and is set down at the right hand of the Throne of God" (Hebrews 12:1-2).

Although the enemy saw me as a prime target for a spirit of anxiety, satan miscalculated. My adversary wanted grief to spiral and become anxiety and to make me apprehensive, fear my future, and dread my outcome. I lamented in various degrees over the loss of my husband and experienced anguish in both my mind and body as I mourned, but never did I look upon my future with uneasiness, despair, or uncertainty. My Lord secured my future. In this truth, lay the devil's misfortune.

> "Faithful *is* He that calls you, who also will do *it*"
> (*1* Thessalonians 5:24).

Satan's attempt to push me towards doubt, fear, and anxiety failed and instead bereavement caused me to thrust myself into the Father's arms, sit in His lap and not get up, and grab hold of Jesus and not let go. God knew what my response would be and just allowed the enemy to test my faith. Mourning did not cancel my salvation, eliminate faith, remove God's love, nor define my destiny. Satan tried to instill fear that what I pressed towards I could not attain and did not even exist. The devil desired me. God in contrast wanted to perfect me in His love and attain movement towards my preordained future, not the demise the enemy wanted.

"There is no fear in love; but perfect love casts out fear: because fear has torment. He that fears is not made perfect in love"
(1 John 4:18).

"But the fearful, and unbelieving, and the abominable, and murderers, and whoremongers, and sorcerers, and idolaters, and all liars, shall have their part in the lake which burns with fire and brimstone: which is the second death" (Revelation 21:8).

My advancement in the perfection process, although full of difficulties, accomplished what God intended it to do. I saw my eternal life with my Lord Jesus the Christ—justified, saved, called according to His purpose, conformed to His image, glorified, perfected, sanctified, an overcomer, inheritor of all things, and a son of God (Romans 5:8-9; 8:28; 1 Corinthians 15:49;

2 Thessalonians 1:11-12; Hebrews 10:14; Revelation 21:7). Life on earth, be that as it may, was something I had to endure; and the magnitude of grief that I had never experienced before was a journey to get through. But faith gave me victory to overcome the depths of my mourning. Faith enabled me to overcome anything life threw my way. By faith, I escaped the emptiness left by my husband's departure and persevered through bereavement. Faith ensured I overcame all things and inherited the promise of God: All things. This is what the tempter wanted to demolish, my faith.

> *"There has no temptation taken you but such as is common to man: but God is faithful, who will not suffer you to be tempted above that you are able; but will with the temptation also make a way to escape, that you may be able to bear it"* (1 Corinthians 10:13).

I visited my beloved's gravesite for the first time on September 12th—255 days after he departed. I placed a small rock on his headstone, which was a Jewish custom I heard about that indicated someone had visited the grave.[4] Moved by the custom, I decided to follow this tradition. I also blessed his bones and left quickly after I took a couple of pictures. A bee buzzed around me and would not leave me alone. Not amused at the time, later I laughed and imagined Ron as he looked at me and said, "There she goes again; can't stand still because of a bee." If outside with me, he tried to encourage me to not hop and flap my arms but just gently wave it away. Otherwise, he looked out a window and just shook his head at me as I danced and flung around. I learned to come in at pollen collection time or go to a different area of the yard. I observed their feeding cycles. I had gotten stung once by something and examined my arm to try and find the teeth that gripped my flesh. That is what it felt like, and never did I want to experience that sensation again.

Filled with emotion, however, I left the cemetery and sobbed all the way home,

---

[4] Yehuda Shurpin, "Why Do Jews Put Pebbles on Tombstones?"
https://www.chabad.org/library/article_cdo/aid/3002490/sc/pt_share/jewish/Why-Do-Jews-Put-Pebbles-on-Tombstones.htm.

upset that I let a bee make me leave before I intended to go. But I realized that the bee, though a nuisance, served as an excuse for my abrupt departure. I missed my husband, and his absence tormented me. I could not claw myself down into his grave, cling to his bones, and get relief from my pain. The visit provided no consolation. I could not bear the comprehension of his absence and the void I felt. I realized only Christ could bring me comfort. I never visited his gravesite again. Nor have I driven down the street pass the entrance to the cemetery. I have gone a different way.

I purchased the deed to the plot next to my beloved. I bought it at the same time I acquired the deed to the spot where I buried his casket. Perhaps it was a sales tactic of the funeral home. Nevertheless, at the time, I wanted my bones to lie next to his. I did not buy a double headstone to add my name later. However, in my will I have requested that if I am out of the country and the cost to bring me home is too expensive that I be buried in the country where I died because that is where God sent me. I honored my beloved's bones with a blessing and tombstone, just as Jacob honored

Rachel with a pillar; and I gave instructions for my bones, as Jacob and Joseph did theirs, in my will (Genesis 35:20; 49:29-30; 50:25).

Chapter 5

Offense

*"The Spirit of the Lord is upon me;
because the Lord has anointed me
to preach good tidings unto the
meek; He has sent me to bind up
the brokenhearted, to proclaim
liberty to the captives, and the
opening of the prison to them
that are bound; to proclaim the
acceptable year of the Lord, and
the day of vengeance of our God; to
comfort all that mourn; to appoint
unto them that mourn in Zion, to
give unto them beauty for ashes,
the oil of joy for mourning, the
garment of praise for the spirit of
heaviness; that they might be called
trees of righteousness, the planting
of the Lord, that He might be
glorified"* (Isaiah 61:1-3).

In my grief journey, I discovered that because
someone could preach, pray, or evangelize it

did not necessarily mean they could bind up the brokenhearted, comfort those that mourn, give mourners beauty for ashes or the oil of joy in place of lamentation, clothe bereavers with garments of praise instead of being clothed with a spirit of heaviness, nor position those in anguish to be trees of righteousness planted by the Lord to glorify Him. God showed me His viewpoint of offense and that He did not anoint everyone to heal those in pain over the departure of their loved one.

I struggled to express what happened to my husband. I came to understand that my search for words to vocalize my sorrow had the subconscious plan to elicit a response that would alleviate my pain. If I described Ron's state as died, dead, or deceased, I thought it would sound harsh, cold, and evoke shock—not empathy. Besides, I hated to use those terms. I believed in the biblical truth: To be absent in the body was to be present and alive in Christ (1 Thessalonians 5:9-10). I envisioned my beloved's spirit with Jesus, separated from rotting flesh and bones. My certainty of Ron's destiny brought me comfort. However, the disruption of my life caused by his departure produced agony. Crushed by grief, my hopes for our future together on earth was demolished. I suffered loss of what could have been—what we were moving towards. In a whirlwind of torment and in desperation, I sought release from anguish and relief from aloneness. Although I cried out daily to God, I also looked to friends, family, and those in ministry for help.

One day, I attended a home prayer meeting. I knew all who were there. We had prayed together for years. Before the meeting started, we greeted one another in the usual expressions of salutations. I mentioned to a couple that I had lost my husband. The man laughed and asked, "Where did he go?" and "Did you find him?" Surprised by his comment, I withdrew. I do not know if he ever said, "I am sorry for your loss." I could not grasp why he laughed. I did not enjoy the trivialization of my husband's departure nor his offhandedness and laughter. Even though others talked and some (him included) looked at me, I did not hear nor respond. I focused to conceal a gamut of emotions.

Sensations of exposure, hurt, unimportance, embarrassment, and shame washed over me. I told myself that I should have kept my mouth shut. His calloused lack of decency in response was not something I caused. I had reached for comfort and received laughter. In silence, I chastised myself for my expectation of sympathy and faulted those around me for their deficiency thereof. I wanted to bolt, but I stayed.

I asked the pastor of the prayer group if he and his wife could talk with me. I reached out to them because of their position and our friendship. Bereavement hindered my life and I anticipated that they could guide me out of my torment. He indicated that he would get back to me. In desperation, I thought I would hear back from him later that day; instead, he called the next day.

He indicated that his wife said she could not help me, but he would talk with me. I said that I no longer needed his help; the Holy Spirit answered my cry and eased my anguish. As I hung up, I thought, "If I had contemplated suicide, I would be dead." I did not understand his wife's position. His slow response and her stand caused me to shun them. I could not comprehend our past friendship and fellowship. I felt neglected, and the hope of outpoured human love upon me shattered.

But as I continued with my journey of mourning and listened to the Holy Spirit woo me to see God's perspective, He revealed that I looked for and sought comfort where I would find none. I longed for the Word to be activated in my life as I hoped others would use their wisdom, teach me how to overcome my torment, and put in my mind and heart the psalms and hymns that would bring deliverance to my life (Colossians 3:16). I yearned for effectual fervent prayers that would break the bondage of grief (James 5:16).

God wanted me to depend on Him as my healer and trust Him to send the person He chose to minister empathy. And He did send. When I had intense episodes of mourning, I received calls. Someone I encountered with brevity requested confirmation from me in regards to my husband's departure; and instead of a verbal response, I received a hug. Another I interacted with as I managed financial matters sent me a box of brownies on my first Valentine's Day without my husband. The calls from a dear friend, the hug, and the brownies exemplified God's power and presence because I felt better afterwards.

Any individual who did not lessen my pain I could not fault. I had sought the wrong source. I had pursued comfort, deliverance from grief, and help to mend a broken heart from people God had not separated and chosen to give what I desired. Disappointment occurred because I thought they should have provided what I needed, and I was discomforted because I did not receive what I expected. Because they could not help me with relief, I ceased to fellowship with them. However, my analysis and subsequent reaction included flawed assumptions. I discovered that everyone who attempted to guide me out of my sorrow had not received that gifting of healing virtue from God to do so and that the Lord did not minister through everybody who spoke.

God reminded me that He anointed Jesus with the Holy Ghost and with power. Because of that anointing, Christ went about and did good and healed all that were oppressed of the devil for God was with Him (Acts 10:38). If Jesus was anointed by God to heal and deliver, man also had to be purposed and set aside by the Father to render deliverance in Jesus' name. Only the anointing from God could break the yoke from the impact of bereavement (Isaiah 10:27).

I have heard many leaders in ministry advise, "Do not go outside of your anointing." This was a double-edged message that I surmised warned: Don't attempt to do what the Lord has not chosen you to do, and don't seek help from someone God has not set aside to minister what you need. The pastor's wife who said she could not help me knew her boundaries. It had nothing to do with our friendship, love, or fellowship. Jesus also knew the timing of her husband's call. Perhaps he, too, although outside of his ministry tried to offer help. But Jesus, the Anointed One answered my cry and calmed my spirit before he called.

To provide an example of a different view of offense, the Holy Spirit directed me to the story of when Jesus' parents were offended by Him in Luke 2:42-52. Joseph and Mary discovered the absence of their 12-year-old son as they traveled with others back to Nazareth. They returned to Jerusalem in torment to look for Jesus. They located Him after a three-day search. Mary asked her son how He could do such a thing, staying behind and bring His father and her anguish as they sought His whereabouts. Jesus responded with a question to His mother, "Why is it that you looked for me when you should have realized I must be about my Father's business?" Nevertheless, though Joseph and Mary did not understand, Jesus in obedience returned home with His parents. Even though He had amazed those at the temple where His parents found Him, He knew that the time of His power had not yet come.

The Holy Spirit showed me that I, like Jesus' parents, had anticipated but did not get what I expected. Joseph and Mary did not foresee nor understand their son's behavior. His action discomfited them. I, too, in many cases did not comprehend the response of those I approached for empathy and as a result suffered increased pain.

The Spirit of God also showed me those I sought were like Jesus, going about their Father's business. Just as Jesus increased in wisdom, stature, and favor with God and man as He went about and did the Lord's will, those I looked to were doing the same as they promoted the kingdom of God on the earth according to the will of the Father for their lives (Matthew 6:10; 7:21). Our perfection process and journey to our destiny, the kingdom of heaven, took different paths as the Father's will for them did not include ministry to me. I faced offense on my road to blamelessness.

"Woe to the world because of offenses! For offenses must come, but woe to that man by whom the offense comes!"
(Matthew 18:7, NKJV)

My focus shifted. I determined to understand and surrender to the Lord's desire—to rid my life of the dross of displeasure in others. It no longer mattered what I did not receive from others. I became excited about what God schooled in me, which was the continued manifestation of the mind of Christ through deliverance from offense. It was a journey through grief headed towards perfection.

"For who has known the mind of
the Lord, that he may instruct him?
But we have the mind of Christ"
(1 Corinthians 2:16).

Although God used those He anointed to ease my pain, He wanted me to come to Him for my relief that came from comprehension of what He taught me through life without my beloved husband. He put the spotlight on me to reveal where my faith lacked obedience to the Word of God. When I went to others whom I thought could and should help me and they did not, I felt betrayed, scorned, and as if I had a plague. However, in my heart I had the sin of offense.

I repented. I had to exercise myself to always have a heart and mind void of dissatisfaction. I realized that I held myself in captivity to lamentation not because of what others did or did not do but by what I did in ignorance of God's blueprint for Christlikeness as I mourned. The spirit of displeasure that I allowed to stumble into my heart had to be removed just like the spirit of grief that caused torment. Offense enhanced and did not diminish anguish.

"And herein do I exercise myself to have always a conscience void of offense toward God, and toward men" (Acts 24:16).

I cast down the clutter of negative thoughts and love came forth for the brethren whom I thought disregarded or ignored me and did not give me what I perceived I should have received from them.

"And the peace of God, which passes all understanding, shall keep your hearts and minds through Christ Jesus. Finally, brethren, whatsoever things are true, whatsoever things are honest, whatsoever things are just, whatsoever things are pure, whatsoever things are lovely, whatsoever things are of good report; if there be any virtue, and if there be any praise, think on these

things" (Philippians 4:7-8).

Chapter 6

Joy Stealers and Widow Killers

The enemy wanted to bring me to a state of exhaustion and lifelessness where the devil could attempt to rewrite my past, present, and future. Satan's assault included the manipulation of people who besieged me with the intent to intensify my grief so that faith, hope, peace, and strength would depart. I called these people joy stealers and widow killers—those who tried to bring me down to their level, in their mire muck, rather than come up to my faith stance. It was the epitome of misery loves company. At times, it seemed as if a deluge of negative people full of complaint, murmuring, unforgiveness, and fear were sent my way.

I encountered some people that helped me; however, others clung to me as if I was their lifeline. Some dumped their problems on me as they would waste in a toilet. Others wanted a handout. Some shunned me, and others—even those in ministry—admitted they could not help as they said, "It's too much for me." Others judged my lamentation. One person told me that I had time to get adjusted to my beloved's death (a sudden death was depicted by them as harder). However, I explained that Ron's departure was an abrupt death to me because I never expected it to happen. I had the assumption that his body would be normalized—either by a miracle, medicine, or combination of both. I responded that I never accepted man's prognosis and one-year life expectancy.

Afterwards, I recalled that they had experienced a quick and unexpected death, but I concluded that never would I assign a level of sorrow or diminish how someone mourned. I commented to myself that they had no right to categorize my bereavement nor judge how I grieved. But the deceiver had blinded them to this truth and tried to use this mindset as an oppression tactic. The enemy attempted to instill guilt in regards to my depth of anguish rather than comfort and release from pain. I ignored their consultation because I knew the Lord judged whether I be found faithful during my trial, not the extent of lamentation (1 Corinthians 4:2-4).

I had lived with the expectancy of Ron being healed, so to me his death occurred without warning. Because I was not prepared for this occurrence, it seemed as if a wreck happened. My mind had focused on the care of Ron just as I would a sick child. I monitored his illness, provided help where needed, and waited for the sickness to be gone from his body. Just as I did not expect to be killed in a car crash, or by an icicle that fell from a tall building with the impact of a microwave oven hitting me in my head as I walked down the street, or by a tornado that ripped me apart or caused my home to cave in on me, or by a tsunami that washed me out to sea never to be seen or heard from again, or being at my desk when a heart attack caused my body to cease functioning, I did not expect my husband's bone marrow to dry up nor cancer to consume his body with the result that it could no longer provide a vessel for his spirit. All of these examples caused lives to cease contrary to expectation and initiated shock for those left behind.

I had the same reaction to my beloved's departure as I did when I saw my 2-week-old son's spirit leave his body at 4:00 a.m. and fly out through the ceiling. If I had not been holding him to burp and he had been sleeping in his bed, it would have been a case of sudden infant death syndrome (SIDS).[5] But I screamed for the Lord to put him back. The paramedics came; and although I did not see Chris re-enter his body, his dad and the paramedics resuscitated him several times.

I experienced the same trauma when Ron left his body as I did at the sudden departure of my son. Though I cried out for both, God chose to return one. My spirit remembered the stories I had heard of how others who were sick had left their bodies but returned. Some returned to a healed body; others returned to a trial through pain and recovery period until they arrived at a place of deliverance from

---

[5] From Wikipedia, the free encyclopedia: Sudden infant death syndrome (SIDS) is the sudden unexplained death of a child of less than one year of age. Diagnosis requires that the death remain unexplained even after a thorough autopsy and detailed death scene investigation. SIDS usually occurs during sleep typically between the hours of midnight and 9:00 a.m..

sickness or a damaged vessel. With my son, his respiratory system went through seasons of transition attributed to SIDS. I anticipated the same for my husband when I cried out for him to come back. I expected him to come back in wholeness or with movement towards healing but not the permanency of him being gone.

There were people that I thought were friends—my husband and I had visited in their home, we had them in our home, and we had gone out to restaurants and on vacations together—but I never heard from them again. They never acknowledged my calls or offered condolences. The silence was just as painful to endure as an opinion that criticized my mourning.

I discerned my adversary was at work in others and tried to guide them to turn complaint into praise, murmur into thankfulness, unforgiveness into forgiveness, and hate into love (Matthew 6:14-15; 1 John 4:20-21). However, some were so consumed with the enemy's agenda against me—the devil who already had them bound—that they continued to rant, ignore my counsel, and deny the truth regarding their conversation. One person screamed at me, saying that if I could not handle it (their seething complaint regarding another) they would just not talk to me. When threatened with the termination of our friendship, they tried to leverage our fellowship according to their dumping terms. I had to guard my mouth, choose to be slow in response, and in some cases warn that if they did not change their behavior I could not continue to converse with them then or in the future. I stated that I would not let them yell at me nor would I argue with them.

> *"If any man among you seem to be religious, and bridles not his tongue, but deceives his own heart, this man's religion is vain"*
> *(James 1:26).*

I had to block phone numbers or warn more than once to halt the joy stealers' and widow killers' attacks. However, it came to be that most of those individuals stopped being part of my life. I separated myself from them and prayed that God would intervene in their lives and bring about deliverance.

"Let no man deceive you with vain words: for because of these things comes the wrath of God upon the children of disobedience. Be not you therefore partakers with them. For you were sometimes darkness, but now are light in the Lord: walk as children of light: (for the fruit of the Spirit is in all goodness and righteousness and truth;) proving what is acceptable unto the Lord. And have no fellowship with the unfruitful works of darkness, but rather reprove them"
(Ephesians 5:6-11).

I denied satan's maneuver to cause me to sin with thoughts, words, or deeds attributed to works of the flesh; instead I continued movement towards my perfection process and journey through grief with demonstrative fruit of the Spirit evident in my life. I determined that I would not let anyone speak death upon me for life and death resided in the tongue (Proverbs 18:21). I chose to live and partake of life and to not be deterred by joy stealers and widow killers.

"For in many things we offend all.
If any man offend not in word, the
same *is* a perfect man, *and* able
also to bridle the whole body.
Behold, we put bits in the horses'
mouths, that they may obey us; and
we turn about their whole body.
Behold also ships, which though
they be so great, and *are* driven of
fierce winds, yet are they turned
about with a very small helm,
whithersoever the governor lists.
Even so the tongue is a little
member, and boasts great things.
Behold, how great a matter a little
fire kindles! And the tongue *is* a
fire, a world of iniquity: so is the
tongue among our members, that
it defiles the whole body, and sets
on fire the course of nature; and it
is set on fire of hell. For every kind
of beasts, and of birds, and of
serpents, and of things in the sea, is
tamed, and has been tamed of
mankind: but the tongue can no
man tame; *it is* an unruly evil, full
of deadly poison. Therewith bless

we God, even the Father; and therewith curse we men, which are made after the similitude of God. Out of the same mouth proceeds blessing and cursing. My brethren, these things ought not so to be" (James 3:2-10).

Chapter 7

Encourage Yourself
and Praise the Lord

I encouraged myself in the Lord as I experienced setbacks in my journey through sorrow due to the departure of my husband. I depended upon and expected God to get me through bereavement and bring me into a place of peace and victory over mourning. During my most intense lamentation periods, the Holy Spirit directed me to examples in the Bible where Israel had to hearten themselves in the Lord, offer themselves for His purpose, and praise God as they waited for the promised success in a battle.

I found solace in Judges 19 and 20. These chapters tell of the occurrence where a Levite went after his unfaithful concubine who had left him and sought refuge in her father's house. After he gathered her, on the way back home they stayed in a city that belonged to the tribe of Benjamin.

Benjamite men came to the home where they lodged and demanded that the master of the house give them the Levite so that they might know him. The Levite gave these men his concubine instead, whom they abused all night. In the morning after her release, she stumbled back to the house and dropped dead at the door. After the Levite discovered his concubine's body, he took her home and cut her up into 12 pieces. He sent the body parts throughout Israel.

After this, all the tribes gathered in an assembly and the Levite told them about the deeds of the Benjamite men. He requested their advice and counsel as to what should be done concerning the matter. Men of the tribes went to the city where Benjamite men perpetrated the evil act and told them to give up the guilty men to be put to death. But they refused and chose instead to go to war against their brethren.

The children of Israel asked God who should go out to battle first against Benjamin. God responded, "Judah" (Judges 20:18). The tribe of Benjamin, however, won the first battle and killed thousands of their Israeli brothers. But the children of Israel encouraged themselves, wept, and again asked counsel of God whether or not they should go to battle against Benjamin. God said, "Yes, go up against them" (v. 23). Yet, the tribe of Benjamin triumphed again on the second day and killed thousands of their brethren.

The children of Israel wept, fasted, offered burnt and peace offerings to the Lord, and then asked again if they should battle against their brothers or cease. The Lord said, "Go up; for tomorrow I will deliver the children of Benjamin into your hand" (v. 28). The next day not only did they have victory over the Benjamite men of war, but they set fire to the city where the crime took place and sought after the children of Benjamin who escaped the battle, killed them, and burned every city that gave them refuge.

The tribe of Benjamin who had caused pain to the Levite, death to his wife, and mourning to the other tribes of Israel represented my anguish. In the same way, the spirit of heaviness tried to consume me with torment and snuff out my life. The Holy Spirit presented the analogy that just as more of the children of Israel had to die in battle even when the Lord told them to go to war; more of me had to die as God took me through the trial set before me, which was grief. But just as Israel attained complete success in warfare against the tribe of Benjamin, I obtained victory through the cross. Israel had to encourage themselves in the Lord, believe God for a promised win, and go out to battle again and again until the I Am (Exodus 3:14) moved and delivered defeat of their brethren into their hand. I had to do the same, and believe my Father for conquest over mourning. Every day, I encouraged myself in the midst of my torture that the manifestation of my Lord's truth would occur. Jesus overcame my pain and I had to abide in and assimilate that which He accomplished through His shed blood on the cross.

In this encounter, God sent out the tribe of Judah first. Judah is said to mean "praise" because at his birth, Leah his mother said, "Now will I praise the Lord"; then she gave him the name Judah (Genesis 29:35). Praise (Judah) went out to battle first. The Lord also established that the tribe of Judah would go out first from the camp (Numbers 2:9). Praise always went before them. Jesus said that He is the first and the last, and He is from the tribe of Judah (Matthew 1:1-16; Revelation 1:11). God set forth throughout scripture the testimony of His Son Jesus, the Spirit of Prophecy (Revelation 19:10). When Jacob blessed his son Judah, he prophesized that his brethren would praise him, his hand would be on the neck of his enemies, all of Jacob's children would bow down before him, the scepter would not depart from him, and people would be gathered unto him (Genesis 49:8-10). The Holy Spirit emphasized an example of the character of Christ given in scripture through Judges 20 and Numbers 2 that He is the first, the beginning, and the Word of God (John 1:1; Revelation 19:13).

I applied the blessings of Judah and Spirit of Prophecy to my circumstance of lamentation. I recognized that Jesus went before me as I entered the grief battle, Christ abided in me and walked with me as I endured anguish, and my Savior assured the manifestation of the Word of God in me that He overcame my pain at the cross. I praised Christ at the beginning of my journey of mourning, praised Him through torment, and praised Him when I received relief.

> *"By Him therefore let us offer the*
> *sacrifice of praise to God*
> *continually, that is, the fruit of our*
> *lips giving thanks to His Name"*
> *(Hebrews 13:15).*

I proclaimed the first and the last over and over again, for it took more than one affirmation to become victorious over sorrow of my husband's departure and establish the "it is finished" for my pain as declared by Christ on the cross (John 19:30). Strengthened by the example when men of Israel had to encourage themselves for warfare even after they had lost, I was inspired by the Lord to fight the spirit of anguish until I personified victory. I realized that my confrontation with deprivation belonged to the Lord and not to me. I willingly offered myself to Him to do whatever He needed to do in me to bring me to a place of peace and success over grief.

The Holy Spirit also spoke to me through Jael's actions. Her deeds are mentioned in Judges 4 and 5. She willingly offered herself for the purpose of God. Jael took a hammer and tent peg and nailed Sisera's head to the ground and killed the captain of the army sent to destroy Israel. I saw myself as Jael. My weapon not a tent peg but the work accomplished on the cross by Christ who pulled down the stronghold of mourning over my life when He gave up His Ghost. My flesh could not do it, only the crucified Christ. Jesus annihilated my suffering when nailed to the cross, just like Jael destroyed Sisera as an enemy when she hammered his head to the ground.

My adversary wanted lamentation to demolish me—to keep me bound and in a state of perpetual discomfort. Satan wanted to use my anguish to exalt himself victoriously over me, thereby exalting himself over God. I trusted the Lord and let Him show me the path to the manifestation of freedom from bereavement in my life. I ignored the attempts of the enemy to convince me that the possibility of healing from the void left by the departure of my husband did not exist. I sang a song of praise to my Lord and offered myself to God to do as He willed so that I would experience triumph over torment that clung to my mind, body, soul, and spirit.

> "For though we walk in the flesh, we do not war after the flesh: (for the weapons of our warfare *are* not carnal, but mighty through God to the pulling down of strongholds;) casting down imaginations, and every high thing that exalts itself against the knowledge of God, and bringing into captivity every thought to the obedience of Christ; and having readiness to revenge all disobedience, when your obedience is fulfilled" (2 Corinthians 10:3-6).

Chapter 8

I Visited Him in Heaven

"In My Father's house are many mansions: if it were not so, I would have told you. I go to prepare a place for you" (John 14:2).

On the evening of the five-month anniversary of my beloved's leaving, I went to bed and longed for his presence. I awakened (I checked the time at 4:23 a.m. though it may have been five minutes earlier) with the awareness of my spirit re-entering my body. My first thought, which I verbalized and I heard was, "I'm back." Though I did not have cognizance of the hand of God upon me or awareness that the Spirit of God took me, like Ezekiel I knew that I had left my body and returned to it (Ezekiel 1:2-3; 3:12).

In my out-of-body experience, I visited my husband and met him in the lobby of the building where he lived. I perceived we were separated but still married. Going up the elevator, he and I talked about his family. I repeated a conversation I had with them the first week after he departed. I started with, "In January while you were away. . . ." My husband told me how I should respond to their call. As we got off the elevator, I informed him of my response. Relief swept over me as he expressed his approval. We arrived at his apartment. I did not recall the floor, but his apartment door had the number 21. I sensed though that we were in a building with many floors and many apartments on each floor.

I entered his home. Breathlessness overtook me as I looked upon the crisp, clean, and bright colors of my beloved's dwelling place. It was beyond beautiful and just perfect for him. Never had I seen décor like it in person or in any magazine. It had colors of beautiful bright white, vibrant blue, and rich bright deep salmon. My husband loved water, swimming in the ocean, sailing, and snorkeling. It had that kind of feeling—freshness and the atmosphere of peace, beauty, and indescribable awe. His modern habitation had a beautiful white leather couch and huge picture windows. I liked it, but I kept being amazed by how it just spoke Ron. I could think of nothing to add or take away as it seemed to be a perfect place for him.

As I stood in the entrance engrossed with what I saw before me, unexpectedly an attractive woman with long blond hair came in. I perceived she had in her hand a single key, unlocked the door, and just let herself in. Surprised to see me, she immediately started to talk as if she was onsite staff inspecting Ron's apartment. However, I discerned some other agenda. I suspected that she did not just have a "manager's key" but personally had a key to my husband's place. I realized that she had either stirred jealousy in my heart, mistrust, or suspicion regarding the real reason for her visit. I felt threatened somehow by her because although in the spirit I still had a carnal mind. As she spoke, Ron with gentleness told her, "(calling her by name, which I did not recall), you cannot just walk in here."

She looked at me and questioned how we could still act married though we were apart. I went over to Ron and put my arms around him and he put his around me, and

I said, "Because we love one another." My beloved agreed with me and kissed me.

In that moment, I experienced love that upon my return to my body on my bed I could not find the words to describe what surrounded my husband and me and passed between us. What I felt as I interacted with my beloved transcended my perception of purity, depth, joy, contentment, and peace. Notwithstanding in that moment of my visitation, I understood, tasted, and was engulfed by the fullness of God and unconditional love of Christ. Nothing could either be added to nor taken away.

"For this cause I bow my knees unto the Father of our Lord Jesus Christ, of whom the whole family in heaven and earth is named, that He would grant you, according to the riches of His glory, to be strengthened with might by His Spirit in the inner man; that Christ may dwell in your hearts by faith; that you, being rooted and grounded in love, may be able to comprehend with all saints what is the breadth, and length, and depth, and height;

and to know the love of Christ,
which passes knowledge, that you
might be filled with all fullness of
God" (Ephesians 3:14-19).

I looked back at the woman, and her face changed. I noticed weariness, and her eye makeup was smeared. I asked myself, "Had she been crying?" Looking at her, I knew or the Holy Spirit gave me an image in my mind of an unhappy married woman who perhaps had even been abused. I felt compassion and empathy towards her. She left or just disappeared. I did not recall how.

I gazed towards my husband who now sat at a computer. He stated how hard he would work and did not want me to worry. I sensed his considerateness and heartfelt responsibility for me. We cuddled on the couch. Still in my out-of-body experience, I woke up and found myself lying in bed with my clothes on and noticed beautiful blue skies and white clouds outside his window. Next to me Ron slept. I realized I had fallen asleep without being intimate with my beloved. I awakened Ron and with uneasiness asked,

"Did I fall asleep?" and "Why didn't you wake me?" His response without judgment mirrored what I felt before.

Pure love surrounded us. He had no anger, disappointment, or frustration but served as an exemplary of perfect love. I had the unfounded worry of failure to please. I recognized that the intimacy I knew in my body on earth represented a shadow of what I now encountered with my beloved. I thought in my mind that I had spent the night with him but never saw darkness. I recalled that the night before he had told me that we were getting back together, but it would be different. I wondered and wanted to ask him how and what change he looked for in me or what he expected from me, but I did not.

Back in my bed at home on earth, I sensed my own earthly reality. I concluded that though we were apart, we would see each other again.

> *"And they stoned Stephen, calling upon God, and saying, Lord Jesus, receive my spirit. And he knelled down, and cried with a loud voice, Lord, lay not this sin to their*

charge. And when he had said this, he fell asleep" (Acts 7:59-60).

"For as in Adam all die, even so in Christ shall all be made alive" (1 Corinthians 15:22).

"But I would not have you to be ignorant, brethren, concerning them which are asleep, that you sorrow not, even as others which have no hope. For if we believe that Jesus died and rose again, even so them also which sleep in Jesus will God bring with Him. For this we say unto you by the word of the Lord, that we which are alive and remain unto the coming of the Lord shall not prevent them which are asleep. For the Lord Himself shall descend from heaven with a shout, with the voice of the archangel, and with the trump of God: and the dead in Christ shall rise first: then we which are alive and remain shall be caught up together with them in the clouds, to meet the Lord in the air: and so shall we ever be with the

Lord. Wherefore comfort one another with these words" (1 Thessalonians 4:13-18).

Chapter 9

Lust of the Flesh

I missed my beloved every day. I longed for the intimacy and companionship we shared. I cringed though at the thought of my bed being shared with another, even if I could. I crucified and ruled over my flesh as desires arose in me, and I did not let my body manipulate me. I purposed that I would not allow the devil to pressure me into distorting the beauty of God's creation through pleasures of the flesh. I refused to be a slave to my body's sex drive and be a servant to sin (John 8:34).

The Holy Spirit reminded me of what the Apostle Paul exhorted. He stated that the unmarried and widows should remain so; but if they could not contain themselves, it was better to marry than burn (1 Corinthians 7:8-9). Although a widow but also a divorcée, the Word established my ineligibility to remarry (Matthew 19:9). It further established that adulterers and fornicators would not inherit the kingdom of God (1 Corinthians 6:9-10). I chose eternal life rather than eternal burn.

> *"Therefore put to death your members which are on the earth: fornication, uncleanness, passion, evil desire, and covetousness, which is idolatry. Because of these things the wrath of God is coming upon the sons of disobedience, in which you yourselves once walked when you lived in them"*
> *(Colossians 3:5-7, NKJV).*

I discovered the reality that flesh had its own voice. My body remembered the pleasures God designed it to attain and demanded satisfaction. It existed with obliviousness to my lack of spouse position. Sexual desires seemed to be tied to a biological, inward clock that went off when it was time to receive gratification. I compared it to a baby that demanded milk when hungry. Delay increased the infant's discomfort, and the child expressed displeasure with intensity of expression. I craved sexual satisfaction and denial caused frustration.

I knew that mind, body, soul, and spirit were separate but came together in one body of flesh. I learned to battle my body with steadfastness as if it was a separate entity and told my flesh, "You cannot have that which you desire." I made my cells, blood flow, and that which my body craved bow to my command and line up with my spirit and heart that purported to conform to the Word of God. I had to beat my flesh down with my mind even though it tried to rebel against its owner, me. Nevertheless glad to feel alive with pleasure, yet I decided to not be ruled by my flesh but by the Spirit of God and squashed desire for sexual pleasure like a fly.

I had to become a living testimony and triumph over lust. I believed that Christ overcame my weakness of the flesh at the cross and gave me the strength to do so as I rested in and depended on Him. I accomplished perfection of Christ in me when victorious over my carnal appetite. Therefore, I honored my Lord in my denial of want as He purged me of that biological urge. I preferred that Christ be glorified in and through me rather than burn and was secure because I suffered through denial of self that I would reign with Him (2 Timothy 2:11-13).

> "Beloved, I beg *you* as sojourners and pilgrims, abstain from fleshly lusts which war against the soul, having your conduct honorable among the Gentiles, that when they speak against you as evildoers, they may, by *your* good works which they observe, glorify God in the day of visitation" (*1 Peter 2:11-12, NKJV*).

Be that as it may, I did not want to stifle sexual desires that my Father created my flesh to manifest. Instead, I recognized God's hand in bringing me to a place of self-control. Appetites, whether for food or physical gratification, needed to be checked. Perfection dictated deliverance from indulged consumption of my favorite things—for example, eating a bag of chips rather than a serving size in one setting and devouring a batch of homemade cookies or a whole homemade cake over a weekend or a few days represented areas where gluttony prevailed. My Lord wanted to see crucified flesh (the image of His Son) and not lust. My journey through grief helped me to examine the fruit of my spirit and resemblance to Christ.

> *"But the fruit of the Spirit is love, joy, peace, longsuffering, kindness, goodness, faithfulness, gentleness, self-control. Against such there is no law. And those who are Christ's have crucified the flesh with its passions and desires. If we live in the Spirit, let us also walk in the Spirit" (Galatians 5:22-25, NKJV).*

> *"Abstain from all appearance of evil. And the very God of peace sanctify you wholly; and I pray God your whole spirit and soul and body be preserved blameless unto the coming of our Lord Jesus Christ"* (1 Thessalonians 5:22-23).

Chapter 10

The Journey Continued

I came home to an empty house. I had enjoyed a great day spending time with my daughter and grandson. But then here I was again, home on my own. I said to my Lord, "I am hanging on, Jesus; I am hanging on," and I reached for Him. I stated, "Only You can ease this sorrow; only You can hold me and dry my tears." I expressed to Him that I trusted in Him for my outcome and depended on Him to show me the way of my path. I communicated that others did not know my pain and expounded that they were involved in their own lives and living them out. I continued with my conversation and declared, "Only You can reach out to ease my plight—shadows of the past life." I verbalized to my Savior, "Never did I expect that my last years would be alone years." I concluded with the statement, "But, You knew."

I could breathe now. My chest no longer tight, I wondered what had caused the manifestation of constriction in my body. Concerned about my health, I described my condition of tiredness, lethargy, and just not feeling well to my internist. He ran a gamut of tests only to report that they revealed no disease or illness which caused my weakness. I looked at my doctor who had managed my healthcare for decades and sighed. He had been the first to raise a red flag concerning my husband's health and had kept abreast of his status. I held my head down as I realized and admitted that grief caused my torment. Not sick in my body, I failed and allowed oppression to take over my mind. I had dug my own hole to lie down in and die and be buried. I had to battle me.

My doctor, who was also a Christian, knew me as a strong woman of God who was secure in her faith; however, in that moment he also recognized the disappointment I felt in myself that I had allowed bereavement to overcome my faith. The words that followed encouraged me and helped me to rise above my anguish. He said, "Don't beat yourself up about it."

I accepted that God allowed my adversary to buffet me and that I needed my Lord to exalt me over my circumstance. I could not control my situation. I had no power to stop my husband from departing his physical body, and I wanted the sorrow that followed to leave. Although thoughts of failure tormented me and weakness in my mind and body prevailed, I remained strong in my spirit and faith in Christ. That is all I had left: Jesus and His power that rested on and in me. I strove to deny the persecution of grief and allow my Savior to rise within and shine through me. I learned to see the pleasure of my hardship while being confident that God would give me deliverance from it.

> "And He said unto me, *My grace is sufficient for you: for My strength is made perfect in weakness.* Most gladly therefore will I rather glory in my infirmities, that the power of Christ may rest upon me"
> (2 Corinthians 12:9).

However, being a widow did not give me exempt status from the devil. He tried to use widowhood as a doorway to my demise—to steal, kill, and destroy my peace, joy, contentment, and love. But, though I still mourned, I shut the door to satan in the midst of my pain. I reminded myself that no matter what trial, torment, or vexation I went through, Jesus died on the cross for that too, and He suffered so much more.

"Beloved, think it not strange concerning the fiery trial which is to try you, as though some strange thing happened unto you: but rejoice, inasmuch as you are partakers of Christ's sufferings; that, when His glory shall be revealed, you may be glad also with exceeding joy" (1 Peter 4:12-13).

I worshipped through dance and praise, and I praised and worshipped through dance; it always got me through. I sang unto the Lord through tears. I sang unto the Lord upon my bed. I sang unto the Lord as I slept and dreamed. He led me to the right song at the right time. At times, He awakened me with a song of my own in my heart. Satan gathered all of his forces of darkness and tried to block the manifestation of God's glory in me. God used bereavement to strengthen me.

Everything I thought about life did not prepare me for the death of my spouse. Two truly became one (Matthew 19:4-6). Even 553 days—1 year, 6 months, and 6 days (almost 7)—after my husband's departure, my Friday, Saturday, and Sunday evenings were still reminders of date weekends. My beloved and I had our programs that we would watch on Saturday and Sunday evenings. Fridays brought apprehensiveness of the emptiness to follow. I walked through an empty house. I sat alone on Friday evenings and Saturdays beside the fireplace and watched Christmas movies.

The weekends used to be a break from cooking where we enjoyed our favorite eat-in or takeout restaurants. Memories of food we shared at or from a restaurant brought discomfort, so I cooked instead and ate by myself. I set up only one rather than two TV trays. Homemade cookies or a bowl of freshly popped, buttered popcorn lacked fulfillment because the joint participation that brought pleasure no longer existed. I brushed against no hand as I reached for a cookie or a handful of popcorn. I missed a shared laugh, and no one occupied the other side of the couch. I learned to use my hair paddle brush to apply body cream to areas on my back I could not reach. I remembered hearing or reading that when someone loses a limb they still feel the missing body part. That is what I felt—dismemberment or a hole where there used to be substance.

When I thought of traveling solo after my husband departed, it gave me pause. My travel buddy resided in another place. I realized that whenever I traveled before—conference, job, ministry/missions—I always had my husband waiting for me back home, and I usually called (if I could) and checked in at the end of the day. It was that difference I dreaded. Solo meant solo. Not only did I not have a vacation buddy to travel with, I had no one to come back to. Hesitancy mirrored emptiness. I had to rediscover me. No, I had to discover me. Life before bereavement included my husband, children, a pet, and work—which all came before me.

All of my beloved's clothes are gone—either donated or given away during the first two weeks after he departed (except a favorite night shirt of his I still wore). I knew the Word stated women should not wear men's clothes, but his shirt brought me comfort as I snuggled with it and ached for my beloved's caress. Be that as it may, Christ pointed to the Holy Spirit as my comforter and with resolve I adorned Ron's garment with less frequency. God's Word pierced my heart, and now that shirt is relegated to a drawer out of my wardrobe where our son keeps a few items to use during visits.

> *"A woman shall not wear anything that pertains to a man, nor shall a man put on a woman's garment, for all who do so are an abomination to the Lord your God"* (Deuteronomy 22:5, NKJV).

His desk/office area I cleaned out in my first widow year. I did not read his journals or notes scribbled on any pads or pieces of paper. I could hardly read his writing anyway. I teased him that his writing reminded me of a doctor's scribble on a prescription. I respected his privacy still. I knew all I needed to know. I laughed as I remembered that from his hospital bed by the fireplace he had mustered up the strength and questioned why I rummaged through his desk. My answer that I looked for tax documents for our upcoming filing satisfied his curiosity. His desk became mine, and I turned a spare bedroom into a home business office. His plethora of books I have sorted through, donated many to my public library, and deposited others in the book donation receptacle at a local school. Old textbooks, magazines, articles of his interest, and manuals for long gone appliances or electronics were tossed.

It helped my grief process to rearrange furniture and imagine a new layout of my family room where change removed from my mind the image of Ron in his hospital bed, favorite spot on the couch, or his office. I felt as if my redecoration breathed life into an area where the fragrance of departure and emptiness hovered.

I started the task of sorting items put away in those storage areas of the house that I had not touched since they were put there over the years. The process caused tightness in my chest, but I pressed through with rapidness and emptied out bins, shredded, tossed, or marked for donation items of the past that were no longer needed or wanted. I also organized family and vacation photos. I had fun doing that—even though tears were shed as I looked upon pictures that told stories of our life together.

I alone hummed our favorite Christmas songs or picked them out on the piano. Sometimes, I could still hear the pieces he played. I missed Ron's practicing, not just his playing. I grimaced as I remembered my criticism of his habit of going too fast and hitting the same wrong note over and over again. I repented and desired to hear those wrong notes instead of silence. I realized I missed my beloved's soul and spirit and not the piano's sound. Be that as it may, I thought of Ron as a song that could no longer be sung on earth, just remembered, but given a new sound in heaven. As for me, I had to learn a new song here on earth, not of want of that which is gone but of those things yet to come.

"I waited patiently for the Lord;
And He inclined unto me, and
heard my cry. He brought me up
also out of an horrible pit, out of the
miry clay, and set my feet upon a
rock, and established my goings.
And He has put a new song in my
mouth, even praise unto our God:
many shall see it, and fear, and
shall trust in the Lord"
(Psalm 40:1-3).

I shifted focus off myself, and the Holy Spirit started showing me faces of those left behind by their loved ones. I saw their anguish. I saw that they, too, did not expect to be in the place that they were in now. Although grief was fresh for some, for others the years had gone by and they were not able to move on. Somehow, those images gave me relief as I no longer felt isolated but joined into a fellowship by grief. But instead of consolidated sorrow, empathy filled me as I desired to eliminate their discomfort and to bring them to a place of deliverance, peace, and joy in Christ. All that I hoped for myself I wanted others to obtain.

Two years, eight months, and eight days after by beloved's departure, God's Spirit awakened me with a new song in my heart. I recorded it on my phone as it came forth; and I noticed it started with forlornness from a place of focus on self, but my spirit shifted with immediateness to a burden from my Lord for my nation. In other words, the Holy Spirit awakened my spirit and said, "Come up, Nina, to God's eye view and His interest. It is your anointing and destiny to fulfill His will out of the miry clay of grief." God's Spirit spoke to my heart and said, "Lament for my nation and not over Ron who dwells with Christ."

This is a song.
This is a prayer.
Oh God, hear my cry.
This is a song.
This is my prayer.
Oh God, hear my cry.
See my tears,
For the land I love.
Take this burden,
For the land I love.
My heart is heavy,

For the land I love.
This is my song.
This is my cry.
Oh God, heal my land.
This is a song.
This is my prayer.
Oh God, see my love.
This is a song.
This is a prayer.
My God, heal my land.
This is a song.
This is a prayer.
Oh God, heal my land.

Encouraged to shift my focus and mindset, I realized I had to battle back to an existence of thoughts that were off of me and what I missed and on what pleased the Father through alignment with Jesus' desires for the earth. My Savior reminded me: Look to and follow Him; do as He did—nothing but what pleased the Father—and pray as He did that we all may be one as He and the Father are one (John 12:49; 8:29; 17:20-23). I needed to return to the place of the personification of love for my brethren, America, and the nations of the

earth with an outward and upward thinking
that broke out of my deadlock in torment.

Chapter 11

Anybody for Me?

I have come to understand that the answer to the question, "Is there anybody for me?" is, "No, not now." Years ago, during my marriage to Ron, the Holy Spirit pierced my heart with the truth of the Word regarding divorce. I was married before and my ex-spouse was still living when my eyes were opened to the truth that adultery represented the only valid reason for divorce. If the woman remarried, both she and her new husband committed adultery (Matthew 5:31-32). At the time of this revelation, I repented of my sin against God and accepted the truth of His Word.

Now, after the departure of my beloved, the Spirit of God also spoke to me regarding matters of the heart—a future marriage. I realized the possibility of remarriage only existed if I reconciled back with my ex-husband; otherwise, I would commit adultery (1 Corinthians 7:10-11). I knew the truth, and the truth set me free from sin and condemnation (John 8:31-32). The enemy could not steal my position in Christ nor the Word in my heart. I chose to demonstrate the love of God and my victory over the world by living out faith in obedience to the Word of God regarding a future spouse.

Since I am not eligible to remarry because my first husband is still living, I have called it my consequence of sin. The Holy Spirit comforted me with assurance of my salvation but also reminded me that God established a covenant with me that sealed our relationship with promises of blessings for obedience and disinheritance for disobedience (Hebrews 10:35-38; Galatians 5:19-21). The blood of and my faith in Jesus wiped away the sin of remarriage. Though scarlet to the Lord at the moment it occurred, in its place that spot of iniquity became white as snow and the stain of transgression remembered by God no more (Isaiah 1:18; Hebrews 10:15-17). However, repentance and the Lord's forgiveness did not change my divorced and widowed status that has me bound by the Word of God regarding eligibility for another spouse. Forgiveness did not remove the consequence of sin.

To clarify, the Holy Spirit showed me effects of trespasses. Saul's conversion, infilling of the Holy Ghost, and name being changed to Paul did not cause the believers he did much evil to and destroyed to be restored (Acts 9:1-2; 13-14; 17-21; 13:9-10). David's child conceived by adultery with Bathsheba died even after David repented, fasted, and prayed (2 Samuel 11:2-5; 12:14-18). God put away his sin and did not kill him for the murder of Bathsheba's husband, but the child developed sickness unto death (2 Samuel 11:14-17; 12:13). Just as Saul's and David's transgressions impacted lives (including their own), so too did mine.

The wages of my sin—eternal death—were broken by the gift of God, Christ (Romans 6:23). Jesus forgave the woman who committed adultery and was in danger of being stoned, and He told her to go and sin no more (John 8:10-11). Convinced not to waiver, I resolved to remain in obedience to God's Word, demonstrate rebirth into truth, and keep myself from committing adultery again. The old me died, and I am a new creation in Christ (2 Corinthians 5:17).

"We know that whoever is born of God does not sin; but he who has been born of God keeps himself, and the wicked one does not touch him" (1 John 5:18, NKJV).

Chapter 12

Reminiscing

A Reliable Reminder of Trust

I did not anticipate the wonderfulness of my grief journey. I relished a trip down memory lane that invoked an awareness of the remarkableness of my life with my spouse. Watching Hallmark[6] and Lifetime[7] movies were favorite entertainments of most women I knew, especially around Christmas time. I lived the Hallmark or Lifetime movie. My husband honored me. Every birthday, Valentine's Day, Mother's Day, anniversary, and Christmas I not only received a gift or gifts but also at least three dozen roses, sometimes more (except on Christmas). In addition, I always received

---

[6] From Wikipedia, the free encyclopedia: The Hallmark Channel is an American pay television cable channel with programming targeted at families.
[7] From Wikipedia, Lifetime Entertainment Services is an American entertainment industry company whose media properties are focused on women.

three cards—one in the morning (before I left for work, prior to his illness), one in the afternoon (placed in my briefcase as a surprise during the day), and another in the evening.

I recalled a day when I cleaned out one of my kitchen cabinets, moving things around between a cabinet and dining room buffet. I came across the one china place setting we had selected and purchased as an engagement present to ourselves with the plan to put place settings on our wedding gift list. My beloved had sat at the dining room table near me but was still doing one of his favorite past-times, reading. I remembered the horrified expression on his face as he looked up at me after I whimsically and gently caressed my cup and commented out loud, "I never got my china set."

We were married at city hall. With no ceremony and no reception, we married on our lunch break and a few days later were off for a two-week honeymoon. I had started to plan a simple traditional wedding but got stressed out—aghast at the cost and plans that had gone from simple to extravagant—

and felt guilty about trying to keep what I had envisioned.

Hearing my comment, Ron had looked as if he thought he had failed me and kept trying to get me to go online and find the china. I did, found it, and said, "No, too expensive." He asked me, "How much?" I told him, and he said, "No problem; buy it."

He really had wanted to do this for me. He wanted to demonstrate his love for me through this purchase like the abundance of flowers. Curious, I looked just to see if the china could be obtained years later, but I really did not want it. For me, it was a silly woman's wedding thing. I mused, "I'd rather put the money on something else we would both enjoy." At our large family gatherings with kids running around, we used paper plates; and I had enough everyday dishes for anything else. It had taken some convincing on my part until I finally saw a look of ease on his face that he had not denied me something I wanted.

My prince charming, Hallmark beau loved me and would do anything for me. He also let me pursue anything I wanted and always encouraged or made suggestions if it would help me attain a goal or desire. He commented one time that I never asked for much and was not ever extravagant. His cards were always perfect, but the best were ones he made himself with words from his heart.

People described Ron as a quiet, gentle man who never raised his voice. I grimaced at images of myself when my temperament lacked perfect love. I regretted and repented as I recalled occurrences when my tongue did not communicate in songs and hymns (Ephesians 5:18-21). I also was filled with sorrow that while he lived on the earth I never called him Lord as Sara did Abraham (1 Peter 3:6). Only after my beloved departed did I bestow this honor. But Ron loved me despite my imperfections. In remembrance of his love and the knowledge that only the Father, Son, and Holy Spirit are perfect, I found peace and comfort. I strived to attain perfection. God has worked on the fireball in me. Explosions are under the blood and remembered no more, erased from existence.

"And you, being dead in your sins
and the uncircumcision of your
flesh, has He quickened together

with Him, having forgiven you all
trespasses; blotting out the
handwriting of ordinances that was
against us, which was contrary to
us, and took it out of the way,
nailing it to His cross; having
spoiled principalities and powers,
He made a show of them openly,
triumphing over them in it"
(Colossians 2:13-15).

I moved from a personal reminder of faith and trust in the promises of God through Christ to application of forgiveness to nations. A healed land is a place that is filled with repentant, humble, God-fearing, God-seeking people. I remembered that I played a part in that which would create a healed world. As I reminisced about life with Ron, the Holy Spirit retold me of my faith and obedience to the Word journey with Him. The Spirit of God revived me with continued application of the Lord's guidance and love in my life. Part of the miracle-working power of Christ in me, the hope of glory, turned me toward Jesus, caused me to recognize my shortcomings and failures in being Christ-like, but at the same time moved me forward in the victory of the cross, His shed blood.

The Holy Spirit also brought to my remembrance the time when the Lord spoke to me as I cried in agony upon my bed regarding what I thought I wanted but did not get from my husband of a couple years. He said, "You love him (Ron) unconditionally just as I love you, and you forgive just as you want to be forgiven." Horrification came as the condition of my own soul filled my mind. That moment changed the viewpoint of my marriage forever. My tears immediately dried up as I, in terror and fear of the Lord, realized that the finger I pointed at my husband had to be turned around to me instead. I needed to change and work on myself and get the speck out of my own eye (Luke 6:41-42, NKJV).

I recognized that we both lacked perfection, but it still took determination to live out the Word of God. To become a manifest son of God, I had to change. But the more I came into an understanding of how much God loved me, the more I understood love. My increased knowledge of love gave me the ability to love with an unconditional love and become more like my Lord. I pondered to grasp that God's thoughts of me were greater than the grains of sand (Psalm 139:17-18). I said to myself and repeated to others, "Do you know how many grains of sand there are in the world? And my Father's thoughts of me are greater than that." I exclaimed, "Oh, if I could love like that."

I desired to resemble God for He is love (1 John 4:8). I imagined and longed for my Father to look upon me and say, "Ah, there is my heritage, my reward" (Psalm 127:3). I imaged that when I went before Christ, He would not speak but my actions would replay as His Word scrolled beside my every behavior in comparison and then pronounced my judgment: Either enter and inherit or depart (Matthew 7:21; 25:34-36, 41-43). His written Word, whom He is, would judge me (Daniel 7:9-10).

Life's trials, at times, enhanced the difficulty to trust God and continue with the struggle to become more like Him no matter what circumstance. Grief provided an example for this quagmire. Years ago, God brought me to a place of the truth regarding trust.

"Thus says the Lord; Cursed be the man that trusts in man, and makes flesh his arm, and whose heart departs from the Lord. For he shall be like the heath in the desert, and shall not see when good comes; but shall inhabit the parched places in the wilderness, in a salt land and not inhabited. Blessed is the man that trusts in the Lord, and whose hope the Lord is. For he shall be as a tree planted by the waters, and that spreads out her roots by the river, and shall not see when heat comes, but her leaf shall be green; and shall not be careful in the year of drought, neither shall cease from yielding fruit" (Jeremiah 17:5-8).

The word "cursed" in Jeremiah 17:5 is the Hebrew word *'ārar (aw-rar')*, which means to bind with a spell, to hem in with obstacles, to render powerless, or to resist.[8] Faced with the departure of my husband, I

---

[8] *Word Study Series: The Complete Word Study Old Testament,* General Editor, Warren Baker, D.R.E., Lexical Aids to the Old Testament, #779.

clung to God. This was second nature to me because I had learned to trust the Lord; therefore, I threw myself upon Him. I expected that He would do all He said and would come to my aid. I would not be bound with a spell, hemmed in with obstacles, or rendered powerless by enemy forces. My Father did not throw me into a parched wilderness place but poured out His Spirit upon me like rain so I would be like a well-watered tree, green and fruit yielding.

Mourning, a horrible burden to bear, resembled a heavy weighted presence upon me that crushed the very breath out of me. That sorrow belonged to Christ for God nailed it to His cross. I shifted it back to its place of triumph, and living waters gushed forth from me. My Savior gave me peace, joy, and contentment; and He anointed me in the midst of my pain to bring life, comfort, and joy to others. I needed prayer, but so many others needed my prayers: Nations, people, people groups, and entities.

"Surely He has borne our griefs,
and carried our sorrows: yet we did

esteem Him stricken, smitten of
God, and afflicted. But He was
wounded for our transgressions, He
was bruised for our iniquities: the
chastisement of our peace was
upon Him; and with His stripes we
are healed" (Isaiah 53:4-5).

As anniversaries, birthdays, and holidays rolled by, I missed the flowers, the candy, and the gifts that I said were too much. I understand now Ron's expression of love for me through them. The beauty of the flowers exemplified the beauty he saw in me. The abundance of gifts and cards represented the extravagant love he had for me. The jewels he gave were the twinkle in his eyes and the reflection of the love in his heart. It gave him joy to see the sparkle on me that embodied the fire in his heart for me.

The excitement in his eyes as he gazed at me is missed. In retrospect, I realized that only a love-filled heart could glisten in a man's eyes. Not lust, but love. I considered how my husband and I interplayed with one another and concluded that the love poured out to me from Ron's heart fulfilled me more than pleasures of the flesh. I repented for complaining of the extravagance and the chore of having to arrange so many flowers and clean up afterwards instead of reverencing the love shown by my husband through these gifts.

At times, however, during agony of grief, I wondered if I punished my husband through lack of appreciation for his gifts because of the absence of verbal intimacy I craved. I longed to hear my beloved speak what I saw in his eyes as he looked at me. I yearned for him to articulate his heart for me. But I learned years ago that if I critiqued his communication effort or skill the sparkle in his eyes would dim and he would withdraw. Be that it may, while we were together on earth and as I mourned his departure, the Holy Spirit reminded me of God's Word concerning Eve, the mother of the living (Genesis 3:20). That Word applied to me, and my desire would be to my husband.

"Unto the woman He said, I will greatly multiply your sorrow and your conception; in sorrow you

shall bring forth children; and your
desire shall be to your husband, and
he shall rule over you"
(Genesis 3:16).

I contemplated the word "desire" in
Genesis 3:16, which is translated from the
Hebrew word *tesh-oo-kaw'*. It has the
meaning of stretching out after, a
yearning, or a longing.[9] God ascribed this
to wives this pining for their husband. I
came to understand that my perfection
process not only took place during my
marriage, but the lessons taught by the
Holy Spirit continued in depth as I journeyed
through mourning. I had to move past the
regrets mindset. I repented for feelings and
thoughts of lack of verbal intimacy and
communication neglect by my husband
during my marriage. The Holy Spirit showed
me I erred in this perceived oversight
because, after all, my beloved had never
spoken an unkind word to or about me.
Neither did he question or criticize my

---

[9] *Word Study Series: The Complete Word Study Old
Testament,* General Editor, Warren Baker, D.R.E., Lexical
Aids to the Old Testament, #8669.

ability to express myself. He admired my capability to do so in whatever arena.

Bereavement tested and reminded me of instructions received from the Lord. I determined to assert not only Mary's (the mother of Jesus) statement, "Be it unto me according to your word" attitude but also the nature of Christ (Luke 1:38). I prayed to God, "Take lamentation from me," but like Jesus I said, "Nevertheless, not my will but yours, Father to accomplish in me what You have purposed to be" (Luke 22:41-42).

Ron, in contrast to me, had a meek and quiet spirit. As I reminisced about my life with my husband God reminded me of His viewpoint.

"Blessed are the meek: for they shall inherit the earth"
(Matthew 5:5).

"Whose adorning let it not be that outward adorning of plaiting the hair, and of wearing of gold, or putting on of apparel; But let it be the hidden man of the heart, in that which is not corruptible,

125

even the ornament of a meek
and quiet spirit, which is in the
sight of God of great price"
(*1 Peter 3:3-4*)

The word "meek" in both verses is
translated from the Greek word *praus*
(*prah-ooce'*).[10] The definition refers you to
see the word *prautēs* (*prah-oo'-tace*).

> The definition of *prautēs* states
> that meekness is expressed not in
> a man's outward behavior only,
> nor in his relations to his fellow
> man nor his mere natural disposition;
> but it is expressed rather as an
> inwrought grace of the soul that is
> first and chiefly directed toward
> God. It is the attitude of spirit in
> which one accepts God's dealings
> with them as good and does not
> dispute or resist. It states that,
> according to Aristotle, it is the
> middle course in being angry,
> standing between two extremes:

---

[10] *Word Study Series: The Complete Word Study New Testament,* Executive Editor, Spiros Zodhiates, Th.D., Lexical Aids to the New Testament, #4239.

getting angry without reason and not getting angry at all. It concludes, therefore, that meekness is getting angry at the right time, in the right measure, and for the right reason. It is a condition of the mind and heart that demonstrates gentleness not in weakness but power. It is a virtue born in strength of character.[11]

The phrase "of great price" in 1 Peter 3 was from the Greek word *polytelēs* (*pol-oo-tel-ace'*) and meant extremely expensive, costly, and very precious.[12] God took me to the school of understanding. This section of scripture did not just refer to wives but also applied to all mankind. My husband, who never raised his voice, exhibited anger as composed displeasure. He had virtue born in strength of character that displayed meekness and quietness of spirit. My

---

[11] *Word Study Series: The Complete Word Study New Testament,* Executive Editor, Spiros Zodhiates, Th.D., Lexical Aids to the New Testament, #4240.
[12] *Word Study Series: The Complete Word Study New Testament,* Executive Editor, Spiros Zodhiates, Th.D., Greek Dictionary of the New Testament, #4185.

beloved possessed qualities that were very precious to the Lord and thereby viewed by God as expensive. Sacrifice of self was his cost. Ron never thought of himself higher than he ought to think or gloried in his gift of intelligence (Romans 12:3; 1 Corinthians 4:7).

I paused and asked to no one but myself, "Did the Lord have to take my beloved to make me see the flaws in my character as it concerned meekness and quietness of spirit?" I had a "woe is me" moment (Isaiah 6:5). Meekness and quietness of spirit represented virtues that could be enhanced in me and personify more Christ-like behavior. I also asked to no one but myself, "Did God have to cause the magnitude of grief I experienced to bring me to a place of truth of the condition of my spirit?" Yet I said, "Perhaps He used bereavement as a means to position me to be ready when His Son returns." I answered myself, "I do not know that answer," but it did not matter for I accepted God's will for both me and my husband. I just wanted to be delivered from the anguish, live a life on earth, and perform the will of God for my life. I would not dispute God's acts in my life or

Ron's. I petitioned the Lord to reveal what needed to be changed in me to become like His Son.

> "Teach me, O Lord, the way of
> Your statutes; and I shall keep
> it *unto* the end. Give me
> understanding, and I shall keep
> Your law; yes, I shall observe it
> with *my* whole heart. Make
> me to go in the path of Your
> commandments; for therein do I
> delight. Incline my heart unto Your
> testimonies, and not to
> covetousness. Turn away mine eyes
> from beholding vanity;
> *and* quicken You me in Your way.
> Stablish Your word unto
> Your servant, who *is devoted* to
> Your fear. Turn away my
> reproach which I fear: for Your
> judgments *are* good. Behold,
> I have longed after Your precepts:
> quicken me in Your
> righteousness" (Psalm 119:33-40).

I realized also that love from my husband's heart represented only a fraction of the glimpse of God's love. Intimacy desired from my beloved I determined was only possible with God. The love that enveloped and filled us when I visited Ron in heaven did not exist on earth because we had not been perfected in love. I yearned for that love and saw the glimmer of that love in my beloved because we both resided in love, the Father who is Love (1 John 4:16).

Because I experienced perfect love in my out-of-body visit to heaven, I prayed that others would imagine, know, and believe the love God had for them—even in their own direness, whatever that would be. I hoped that my out-of-body visit would bring knowledge of perfect love to earth as part of my calling to intercede for others. I did not see how anyone could make it through or choose to make it through any trial without God, the Father, His Son, and His Holy Spirit. I endured my trial of bereavement through my journey with God due to my trust in Him. He ordered my footsteps and enabled me to overcome mourning as He kept my feet planted on His path to Him to do His will.

"Hold up my goings in Your paths,

that my footsteps slip not"
(Psalm 17:5).

I have experienced many things in my life—a few that would give some pause: Rape, being held up at gun point, and being escorted off school grounds at a summer camp by a "captain" and put on a bus and told not to come back for three days because a gang rape contract had been put out on me by a rival gang. (I had wondered why a man on the third floor of an apartment building balcony that overlooked the school playground watched me. My assigned guard was a captain in a gang.) I suffered abuse from my ex-husband so strung out on LSD that he would kick me out of bed, awaken me as I slept on the couch with a butcher knife at my throat, beat me in my obviously pregnant belly, pick me up and hold me over our 24th-floor balcony and threaten to throw me off. I gave him our last money—supposedly to go and buy milk for our baby daughter, but he came back with booze. I received a touch from Jesus that stopped blood hemorrhaging and He also normalized my hemoglobin count before a consultation appointment with a bone marrow specialist. I survived three totaled car accidents with no cuts or broken bones, just bruises, and received many more miraculous interventions of God in my life.

Some trials, less or more, others have also endured. Many have been tortured, persecuted, or murdered for faith in Christ. But for me, the worst experience that I have ever gone through was the torment of my husband's spirit, my beloved Ron, leaving this earth. But God caused this disruption in my life. Satan could not do anything to me but what the Father allowed. My trust in the Lord included me asking God through my tears, "What do You want me to learn?" and "What are you trying to show me to bring about the purpose You have for me to accomplish, what I was born for, so that I can hear, 'Well done my good and faithful friend; enter into the kingdom of heaven'? (Matthew 25:14, 21)."

"You are my friends, if you do whatsoever I command you. Henceforth I call you not servants; for the servant

*knows not what his lord does: but I
have called you friends; for all
things that I have heard of My
Father I have made known unto
you"* (John 15:14-15).

Chapter 13

Battle Royal

*"Because You have been my help,
therefore in the shadow of Your
wings I will rejoice. My soul
follows close behind You; Your
right hand upholds me. But those
who seek my life, to destroy it, Shall
go into the lower parts of the earth.
They shall fall by the sword; They
shall be a portion for jackals"
(Psalm 63:7-10, NKJV).*

I had to recognize that not only did I wrestle against myself but also other entities that are not flesh and blood. I fought to not be influenced by principalities, powers, rulers of darkness, spiritual wickedness in high places, and the devil—that tempter and deceiver that desired my demise (Ephesians 4:26-27; 6:12; Luke 4:13; 1 Peter 5:8-9; Revelation 12:9).

I thought that perhaps I had compartmentalized my life. I asked myself if I had reserved God in a section of my life. I questioned whether I had placed my Lord in one box, my life's plans in another, etc. I had believed that I included the Lord in every aspect of my life. "But why," I contemplated, "did grief overtake me when I should have stood in courage?" I thought strength exhibited one of my attributes. I queried how sorrow over my beloved's departure could take me on a journey of torment. I pondered in puzzlement, "Did loss of control over my life propel me into agony?"

Discomfited with myself, I probed why I personified anguish instead of peace and surrender to my Father's will. I did not walk my talk. I felt as if I had entered into a boxing match where my opponent knocked me down. I was not out because I mustered up the strength to stand again; but every time I stood, my challenger struck a blow and I fell. I even saw myself try the rope-a-dope technique.[13] I hung on to my adversary

---

[13] From Wikipedia, the free encyclopedia: "The rope-a-dope is a boxing fighting technique in which one contender leans against the ropes of the boxing ring and draws non-injuring offensive punches, letting the opponent tire themselves out. This gives the former the opportunity to

and waited for the prime opportunity to punch him out.

I came to understand that the boxing ring I entered represented mourning. My assailant floored me over and over with anguish, the spirit of heaviness, and weeping. In times of strength, I clung to the ropes. This action symbolized my cry to Jesus as I held on to Him. However, as I grasped my Lord, waves of sorrow still washed over me as I waited for the chance to annihilate my foe. I also came to realize that the ropes symbolized lamentation that I hung on to like a comfort blanket; it was as if I embraced my beloved as I withstood my enemy's futile blows. But then in comparison to the rope-a-dope method, I knew that my combatant, satan would not tire but planned to continue the attack with the intent to destroy me.

I began to hear the Holy Spirit speak to me what God spoke to Joshua.

---

then execute devastating offensive punches to help them win. The rope-a-dope is most famously associated with Muhammad Ali in his October 1974 Rumble in the Jungle match against world heavyweight champion George Foreman in Kinshasa, Zaire."

"Have I not commanded you? Be strong and of good courage; do not be afraid, nor be dismayed, for the Lord your God is with you wherever you go" (Joshua 1:9, NKJV).

The Lord wanted to prove my faith and remind me that He already defeated my opponent through the blood shed by His Son on the cross. My belief in this truth served as my knockout punch to the devil and deliverance from the pain I incurred because of the departure of my husband. My boxing ring imagery showed me the effects of how the loss of control of my life, plans, and desires supplanted my complete surrender to the "in God, I trust." I surmised that if I had the mindset of total surrender, then I would not have experienced the depth of torment I endured. But God knew the place in my heart that needed to be perfected into His will. And He waited until I came up to His eye view and gave relief and deliverance from my tormentor to thrust me forward into His will.

I determined to become like Phinehas, who with zeal rose up from the weeping congregation of Israel, took a javelin, and killed a man of Israel and the Midianite woman he took into his tent while Israel cried out to the Lord for their sin with the daughters of Moab and their gods. He stayed the plague God caused that had killed thus far 24,000. Phinehas's zealous action for the Lord's sake is told in Numbers 25:1-11. I saw my adversary as that man and woman Phinehas thrust through with a spear and knew I needed to do the same with my knockout punch, the appropriation of the work of the cross.

I also saw my foe as Goliath who defied and taunted the armies of Israel. David was not part of the army but in the camp to bring food to his brethren when he heard Goliath's challenge and asked, "Who is this uncircumcised Philistine that he should dare defy the armies of the living God?" The Hebrew word for "uncircumcised" is *ʿārēl* (aw-rale') and literally refers to the foreskin of the male organ; but as it concerns the attributes of an individual, it pertains to moral and spiritual uncleanness and the inability to hear and hearken to the voice and ways of the Lord.[14]

David confronted Goliath and told him that he would kill him, take his head from him, and give his carcass to the birds of the air and the wild beasts of the earth so that all the earth would know there is a God in Israel who would give him into his hands. David's face-off with Goliath and the gathering of the Philistine and Israelite armies against one another is described in 1 Samuel 17.

I knew that I had to rise up like David in my boxing ring of torment and repel my archenemy's blows rendered in vainness. I had to proclaim, "How dare you come against a child of the living God—the Lord's heritage, His reward. Greater is He in me than you," and punch him out of my life with the declaration of, "The blood of Christ against you uncircumcised Philistine" (Psalm 127:3; 1 John 4:4; Colossians 2:11-15). "My Jesus defeated you on the cross when He said it is finished" (John 19:30).

---

[14] *Word Study Series: The Complete Word Study Old Testament,* General Editor, Warren Baker, D.R.E., Lexical Aids to the Old Testament, #6189.

David's actions showcased God's sovereignty, power, and protection over Israel to their enemy, the Philistines and to all who heard of Goliath's demise and Israel's victory. Just as a boxer defeated in the ring is made a spectacle in the arena, as I overcame my adversary in the boxing ring of anguish, I made a show of his efforts to annihilate me and served as a testimony to all who witnessed my trial of bereavement and deliverance from torment. I displayed God's authority in my life and over my foe as I believed and trusted in Him. As a boxer would obtain the prize and title in a match, I too won the fight in my arena of pain, confirmed the victory of the cross in my life, and pressed toward the furtherance of my perfection process.

At times during my grief journey, I also felt like Elijah and cried out to the Lord, "I alone am left, and my enemy seeks to destroy my life" (1 Kings 19:10). I wailed and exclaimed to myself that I personified zeal of faith, stood with firmness in the promises of the Word, cast down strongholds of unbelief by my husband and others, and demolished truth in their lives did not influence my walk.

God comforted Elijah with the words that there yet remained 7,000 like him who were not killed (1 Kings 19:18). And my Lord also encouraged me and said, "But I have many widows stashed away like you who are my prayer warriors and intercessors that speak my will."

With Elijah, the Father met him, asked "What are you doing here?" and gave instruction as to his next assignment (1 Kings 19:11-13, 15-17). Just the same, the Holy Spirit asked me, "What are you doing, Nina, trudging through grief? You still have work to do." God's Spirit reminded me of what Jesus asked me to do with Him to bring about the Father's will on the earth for Him.

God also demonstrated how to resist my enemy during my time of mourning through visions of the night. In a dream, I saw satan. He looked directly at me from the heavens. He appeared as a very tall, dark-haired man with smooth, flawless pale-white skin, thin but perfectly so, dressed in a black suit and white shirt. Although expressionless, his personification exemplified not just handsomeness but beauty. I remembered commenting to myself, "What a gorgeous specimen of a man." However, I knew his identity and that he focused on me. A group of lions stood in front of him off to his right. One had a large mane. They communicated to both of us. I did not recall what they said, I only discerned a warning given to me. I proclaimed, "No!" as my adversary floated down towards me.

I stood in front of a large picture window inside my apartment home. That entity vanished when just outside the window. I wondered where he went. I walked over to the entry door of my dwelling and looked out the peep hole. He waited outside my door in an upright position with his head down. As he looked up, his eyes revealed surprise that I searched for him. He then appeared immediately inside my home in front of me. I felt that he just floated through the door although I did not see him translate.

My husband and others were in bedrooms down the hall. I cried out to my beloved. I wanted him to come to my aid. I moved towards his bedroom as my enemy floated towards me. When Ron did not answer or come, I cried out to Jesus to help me. As soon as I called on Jesus, the devil immediately disappeared.

The Holy Spirit gave me the interpretation of this vision of the night. I opened the door to satan by my action when I looked for him. That behavior allowed entry into my home. He could not come in unless I turned my attention to him and sought his whereabouts. On the other hand, Christ was my defender, and at His name the devil fled. Man did not answer or help, but my Lord did. The Spirit of God also reminded me by this dream that the enemy, whether he enters my domain or not, is always in observance and waiting for the opportunity to do so. The lions I believe were watchers, letting things play out, and there to witness my faith in action and perfection process.

My adversary had no power over me except that which I gave him by acknowledgment of his existence and the probability of interference in my life. I came to understand the application of the insight of this dream to my journey through bereavement: Stay focused on the battle to get through mourning, cling to Christ, and resist the enemy's attempt to derail God's will for my life. I strived to keep a mindset of no credence given to the influence of my adversary.

God caused grief but did not abandon me during the adjustment trial of life without my beloved. He strengthened, encouraged, and reminded me to stand on His Word and the work of the cross. The Holy Spirit prompted me to concentrate on God's works in the earth and not the adversary for I served the Lord, God of Abraham, Isaac, and Jacob—not satan. I recalled what Jesus said to the devil when the tempter came to Him.

> "And Jesus answered and said unto him, Get you behind me, Satan: for it is written, You shall worship the Lord your God, and Him only shall you serve" (Luke 4:8).

God also brought to my memory His promise of victory through His Son in another dream. This time, satan appeared as a gorgeous black man. I called it the "let's make a deal dream" with a child's life (not mine, but under my care) at stake. The devil told me that either I surrender to him, or he would take the child. I did not say goodbye to the child but did so to others with whom I entrusted the child. As I walked away with my adversary, I questioned his plans for me. He responded that he planned to eat me alive. I continued along for a moment and then looked at him and said, "No, the blood of Jesus against you; the blood of Jesus against you." Before my eyes, he diminished to a puddle of blood.

The scene came to mind of how Dorothy destroyed the Wicked Witch of the West in *The Wizard of Oz*.[15] After Dorothy had been trapped in the witch's castle, that evil being started to declare the demise of Dorothy, the Tin Man, Scarecrow, the Cowardly Lion, and Toto. The witch began with Scarecrow. She lit her broom and set fire to him. Dorothy observed a bucket of water sitting in an opening, ignored the witch's cry to not throw the water, and quenched the fire on Scarecrow's burning arm. Water also splashed on the witch. It immediately started her demise. She cried out, "I am melting, melting,"

[15] *The Wizard of Oz*. Director (primarily) Victor Fleming. Metro-Goldwyn-Mayer (MGM). 1939.

and "Who would have thought that a good little girl like you could destroy my beautiful wickedness?" On the floor, her black hat and other black garments were the only remnants of what had existed. Just as the water destroyed "beautiful wickedness" in the movie, the blood of Jesus destroyed the beautiful devil in my dream. Nothing was left but the blood that overcame evil on the cross.

Both visions of the night served as a reminder that satan had no jurisdiction over me. The devil's attempt to bargain and instill fear was for naught, and his threat to eat me alive was futile. He could not destroy that which did not belong to him; although through his lies, he wanted me to believe that he could.

All of heaven and earth witnessed my journey, battle, and faith walk. God knew He would see faith activated as I moved towards becoming a manifest son of His, which was the prize for endurance and completion of the task set before me: To finish the race to perfection and do God's will for His pleasure. I trusted in the Lord and received the promise of joy. Nevertheless,

I still battled my flesh and principalities to walk out God's love for me.

God foreknew my trial, helped me through it, and proved to be my strength and shield (Psalm 28:7). I just had to suit up with His armor, the Word of God, and remember and live my identity. My Lord wrote my name in His book (Psalm 139:16). He chose me before the foundation of the world and predestined me to be a child of God (Ephesians 1:3-6). Christ, the Lamb slain from the foundation of the world in whose book my name is written, made my individuality by and for Himself (Revelation 13:8; Colossians 1:9-17). The enemy tried to steal, kill, and destroy these truths and demolish my preordained future.

"Trust in the Lord with all your heart; and lean not unto your own understanding. In all your ways acknowledge Him, and He shall direct your paths"
(Proverbs 3:5-6).

"Submit yourselves therefore to God. Resist the devil, and he will flee from you" (James 4:7).

Chapter 14

A Supposed Easy Prey

I discovered that men who I had perceived were a friend to my husband and me or who had been like a brother to me for years without hesitation would pounce on me with lust and the hope of some kind of relationship. One person said, "Any kind of relationship." I had to respond more than once no, and finally forcibly, "Back off!" to one. But again the enemy attacked every way he could—including the use of others that allowed him to do so.

To the man that lurked around a home improvement store looking for a prey, I told, "No, I do not do lunch." At first, I thought he had struck up a friendly conversation in the garden section and wanted my help picking out a fertilizer. Many times, I received and gave gardening advice as I shopped. I discovered years ago that people who loved working outside and gardening have fun sharing at nurseries and home improvement stores. On many occasions, conversations extended to lifestyles, children, and spouses. But in this case, satan beforehand stirred lust in that man's evil heart, and his intent was revealed. He also puffed himself up with self-accolades of position and what he had achieved, and he told me my husband would want me to go out to lunch.

I again refused to give him my phone number and repeated that I would not go out with him. He walked away from me backwards and glared with indignity at the audacity of my rejection. I laughed to myself as I questioned if home improvement stores were now pick-up places. The Holy Spirit reminded me that my adversary walked about seeing whom he could devour (1 Peter 5:8-9). The devil used that man with the purpose to approach, tempt, exploit, and attack me. But I said to myself, "Wrong woman."

Throughout the day, I imagined that man before me and continued our conversation. I pictured myself saying, "Not only do you not know what my husband would want me to do, but you do not even know what he would think. And furthermore," I exhorted as I envisioned our confrontation, "only God or an individual knows the spirit of self within him unless God gives the gift of discerning spirits in others" (1 Corinthians 2:11-12; 12:8-11). I declared as if speaking to him, "My beloved's spirit you cannot discern because he is not here nor did you ever know him." In my mind, I placed that man before me and stated, "I operate in the gift of discerning spirits and what I discern on you are the spirits of lust, murder, thievery, lying, destruction, evil, and fornication." I concluded and dismissed satan's predatory attack by stating as if speaking to that man, "Back to your daddy; I am a woman of God not a foolish woman to be carried away by the wiles of the enemy."

> "A foolish woman *is* clamorous: *she is* simple, and knows nothing" (Proverbs 9:13).

> "This know also, that in the last days perilous times shall come. For men shall be lovers of their own selves, covetous, boasters, proud, blasphemers, disobedient to

parents, unthankful, unholy,
without natural affection,
trucebreakers, false accusers,
incontinent, fierce, despisers of
those that are good, traitors, heady,
highminded, lovers of pleasures
more than lovers of God; having a
form of godliness, but denying the
power thereof: from such turn
away. For of this sort are they
which creep into houses, and lead
captive silly women laden with
sins, led away with divers lusts,
ever learning, and never able to
come to the knowledge of truth"
(2 Timothy 3:1-7).

I recognized that my adversary would use any person or means to derail the righteous walk God set before me and would try to tempt me with relationships to steal God's truth from me. I trusted God to finish the perfection process He started in me and to fulfill the promises of His Word as it concerned me. Like Abram, I believed in the Lord; and what God did for Abram I knew He would do the same for me: Count my faith and trust in Him for righteousness (Genesis 15:6).

Also, a contractor who worked for me discovered my widowhood status and asked me, "Don't you want a man around?" I perceived he wanted to match-make and had inquired not for himself, but he knew a guy. I replied, "No." Respectfully, he never broached the subject again.

My enemy miscalculated again. The light in me, Jesus the Christ, had not dimmed or lost its power. I knew God allowed the encounters with men where lust of the flesh drove their spirit. I believed God spoke of me as He did Job and to satan said, "Have you considered my servant Nina?" (Job 1:6-8). The devil thought he could steal and kill the victory of the cross in me because of the depths of my pain. But my adversary erred. I clung to Jesus with confidence in the promise that my Savior would never leave me nor forsake me (Hebrews 13:5). He would raise me up out of the darkness I wallowed in caused by grief, and I would not fall prey to the captor's will.

"Rejoice not against me, O mine

*enemy: when I fall, I shall
arise; when I sit in darkness, the
Lord shall be a light unto me"*
(Micah 7:8).

I also felt that a relationship with another man would put me in a position of unfaithfulness to my beloved. I knew those thoughts were not truth; but by clinging to the memory of my husband, I created an existence with him based on fanaticism. I still thought of myself as one with him in mind, body, spirit, and soul. I had given myself completely to Ron, and I could not disunite me from him nor did I have any desire to become one with another. Thus, I made myself prey to a false doctrine.

I had to separate myself to live. My foe tried to tempt me to sin and fill the void in my life with another man. However, the Holy Spirit showed me that as I made my departed beloved still a lifeline that I, at the same time, made myself a victim for plunder. I allowed the perceived anchor of Ron to supplant the work of the cross and hinder my walk into the destiny God planned for me on earth after my husband's departure.

My heart shifted to the absolute truth of the Word that my marriage to Ron had ended because in heaven the only marriage would be to the Lamb of God (Luke 20:34-36; Revelation 19:7). I accepted the reality that Ron no longer belonged to me but to Jesus the Christ. Confident that I would see my husband again, not married but joyful together as a bride of Christ, I looked forward to that occasion in whatever heavenly relationship God ordained. It did not matter that we might live apart, each with our own perfect place. But whatever our arrangement, it would fulfill the desire of our hearts as we served, worshipped, and adored our God.

> *"And he showed me a pure river of water of life, clear as crystal, proceeding out of the Throne of God and of the Lamb. In the midst of the street of it, and on either side of the river, was there the tree of life, which bare twelve fruits, and yielded her fruit every month: and the leaves of the tree were for the*

healing of the nations. And there
shall be no more curse: but the
Throne of God and of the Lamb
shall be in it; and His servants
shall serve Him: And they shall see
His face; and His Name shall
be in their foreheads"
(Revelation 22:1-4).

Joy filled my heart as I contemplated our eternal relationship with Jesus and one another. I also experienced delight with the anticipation of us both being with all in heaven and on the new earth in the presence of God, the Father and the Lamb, His Son. In my mind, I placed myself before the Father's throne and for a moment sensed His perfect love that surrounded me. It was that same love I experienced that enraptured me and encompassed Ron and me during my visit with my beloved in heaven.

In my grief, I longed for the love I sensed in heaven and what the Holy Spirit encircled and filled me up with on earth. I could not contemplate any relationship with a man on earth. I knew that no flesh could measure up to or be compared to the agape love that at times engulfed and filled me.

I have heard the audible voice of God. It filled all things that existed—myself included. I surmised that if I am in Jesus and Jesus is in me and Jesus is in the Father with me in Him, then I am in the Father; and as the Father fills all things that exists, so do I (1 John 4:12-13; John 15:5). I thought if the Father is everywhere, so am I because I am in Him. I decided to resemble my Father and not be a prey. Realization occurred that I opened the door to the spirit of victimization. Comprehension came that I made myself captive to an ideology of the past with no regard to my changed circumstance. I put myself in bondage to the spirit of plunder that desired to rob my mind, body, spirit, and soul of all that God intended me to become.

As I looked back at my journey through grief, the Holy Spirit reminded me of Ezekiel who God commanded to prepare and eat a cake made from wheat, barley, beans, lentils, millet, and fitches baked with cow's dung as part of his prophetic act to portray the iniquity of the house of Israel and Judah (Ezekiel 4:9-15). In comparison, I saw that God Himself prepared a cake for me to eat. This cake was not a sign to me of any sin in my life but a means for the Lord to prove me, test me, and cause me to see and live life from a different perspective: His. I came to understand that digestion of God's cake would bring me closer to attaining His purpose, pleasure, and will for my life.

The enemy, through the spirit of prey, tried to add poison unto death to the cake God set before me for my ingestion. The Lord prepared for me a layered cake of grief with filling of promise and icing of blessings. The cake's ingredients were pain, loneliness, unexpectedness, tiredness, tears, and heartache. All of which were manifestations of mourning that consumed me.

As I ate my cake of lamentation, I tortured myself with thoughts of a nonexistent future with my beloved. I gazed forward in time and saw next to me an X-marked spot where my husband should have been, and anguish filled me over the emptiness of that vision. I could not see a new me through the shattered plans and desires my husband and I had for our life together. Satan tried to supplant my invalidated imagery with one that included a pathway to sin through fornication or marriage. The devil hoped to place men he influenced to occupy that X. The Lord, however, replaced emptiness with abundant blessings that He poured over me. I had to acknowledge, believe, and apply who abided with me, filled me, and covered me and in whom I dwelled. God wanted me to recognize my placement in Him.

However, I also sensed God take me— His vessel of honor—break me as a potter does a pot in His hands, and reshape me into a new vessel of love, honor, obedience, and vision. The bombardment of lustful men was nothing compared to the internal sound of being dashed to pieces by the Lord. I learned to see myself as God saw me and gaze into a new chapter of my life that the Lord revealed waited to unfold. God kept His promise and delivered me from evil of being a prey of the terrible and even a prey of my own spirit. He delivered me from being held in captivity.

He contended with those that contended with me.

"But now, O Lord You *are* our Father; we *are* the clay, and You our potter; and we all *are* the work of Your hand" (Isaiah 64:8).

"Then the word of the Lord came to me, saying, O house of Israel, cannot I do with you as this potter? said the Lord. Behold, as the clay *is* in the potter's hand, so *are* you in mine hand, O house of Israel" (Jeremiah 18:5-6).

"Shall the prey be taken from the mighty, or the lawful captive delivered? But thus says the Lord, Even the captives of the mighty shall be taken away, and the prey of the terrible shall be delivered: for I will contend with him that contends with you, and I shall save your children. And I will feed them that oppress you with their own flesh; and they shall be drunken with their own blood, as

with sweet wine: and all flesh shall
know that I the Lord *am* your
Savior and your Redeemer, the
mighty One of Jacob"
(Isaiah 49:24-26).

"And Jabez called on the God of
Israel saying, Oh that You would
bless me indeed, and enlarge my
coast, and that Your hand might be
with me, and that You would keep
me from evil, that it may not
grieve me! And God granted him
that which he requested"
(1 Chronicles 4:10).

Chapter 15

The Depths of Love

During my bereavement journey, the Holy Spirit reminded me of a time years ago when discovery had been made of a huge sapphire and my response to that discovery. I recalled a testimony of a husband-and-wife ministry team that God miraculously gave them jewels. They just appeared. At the time I said, "Lord, You can make that sapphire appear in my hands, or one like it." I thought of the value and what I could do with the money. Then my mind filled with images of publicity and people being thrust into my life because of the gem. I also perceived theft attempts.

On the other hand, as I envisioned the gem in my hands, the Holy Spirit spoke to me and said, "You are more precious to me than that." The Spirit of God told me that my value to the Father exceeded the value of that sapphire. Every time a huge diamond, ruby, or sapphire unearthed, the Lord reminded me that my preciousness to

Him transcended the value of any gem and that His thoughts of me surpassed the grains of sand on the earth (Psalm 139:17-18). God put His love for me in perspective. Nothing on earth mirrored or equaled the Lord's love for me.

My journey of transition through grief taught me a new awareness and depth of love for others. God gave me a new vision as He increased my ability to see love, breathe love, and be love. He positioned me to mirror His Son and do as Jesus did: Only what He saw the Father do and only what personified God—love (John 5:19-20; 3:16). I mused that perhaps God intended for me to see love differently, deepen my understanding of love, and thereby move me closer to perfection of love. I pondered how the departure of my spouse had deepened my love for mankind. As I experienced the loss of the love of my husband, the Father filled the void with His love. However, it represented love not to hold on to but be a conduit for and allow it to flow to others. I learned to let go of that love and become love.

"Beloved, let us love one another:

for love is of God; and every one
that loves is born of God and knows
God" (1 John 4:7).

As I yearned for perfect love with my mind engrossed with thoughts of my husband, I realized God used my bereavement to shift my focus from incomprehension of marriage deprivation and shattering of my lifetime vision to His view of and desire for me. I began to see that God gave me a glimpse and experience of perfect love to provide a demonstration of His embodiment and bring about that same manifestation in me: Perfect love.

"No man has seen God at any time.
If we love one another, God dwells
in us, and His love is perfected in
us" (1 John 4:12).

I thought if I had Jesus in me, I had the power of love, to forgive, show mercy, give grace, and be compassionate. I had sacrifice in me and the illustration of how to offer myself as a living sacrifice. I had in me the One who did only what the Father said, and I purposed to follow that excellence. The

Holy Spirit throughout my journey of grief taught, led, guided, reminded, and quickened in me my predestinate position: To resemble the character of Christ and be a joint-heir as a child of God.

> *"As for me, I will behold Your face*
> *in righteousness: I shall be*
> *satisfied, when I awake, with Your*
> *likeness" (Psalm 17:15).*

In the midst of my pain, I tasted agape love for another. Not that I had never before, but this time it served to rouse me from existence as a bewailer. God opened the door to my heart that held me captive in lamentation to again experience and show His love for others. As I entered a hardware store, a young man standing off to the side of the entrance called out to me to help him obtain a motel room for the night. Parking lots and stores had become a source for con artists to prey upon perceived targets to obtain money. I recognized many from store to store who used the same story time and time again. Some panhandlers made a sizeable tax-free income. But with this young man I felt different.

As I shopped, his image returned to my mind. Upon my exit, I approached him and asked him to repeat what he said. As he spoke, he reminded me of men I visited in prison at a holding facility waiting for trial or transfer to the state penitentiary. One, I recalled, on his first day still in shock from being imprisoned, had on his suit and held a crumbled lunch-sized paper bag with whatever contents he could keep. The young man standing outside the store had that same look. As I took in his appearance, I noticed the tattoos on his neck, ring in his nose, the deflated small backpack on his back that held little if anything, and his clothes that were not quite enough for the cool weather. He appeared to be about the same age as my grandson, perhaps 20 or so.

My heart broke for this child as love poured out from me to him from the Father. I discerned that he experienced an unexpected "suddenly," perhaps being kicked out of his home. Yet I contemplated the possibility of a fraudulent scheme in the works. Even before COVID, I no longer carried a purse—just a couple of credit-card sized wallets in my pockets. However, after COVID quarantine ended, muggings and purse snatchings had become a common threat everywhere. Though I felt compelled to help the young man, I did not because I did not want to reveal the location of my wallets.

Be that as it may, in my car I became overwhelmed by compassion for this child. I drove to the front of the store, beckoned him over to me, and gave him five dollars—not enough for a room but what I had. I carried little cash on me and kept mostly coins in my car. I still remember the joy, surprise, thanks, appreciation, and hope mirrored in his eyes from his heart as the Father's love passed between us. I moved my flesh out of the way and embraced my Lord's will: The kingdom of God on earth—love for my brother.

That act of demonstrated mercy chipped away part of the sorrow that held me in bondage. I discerned a more Christ-like behavior in me as I took the stance that I am on the earth to minister and not be ministered to. With that in mind, I understood God's purpose and will for me regardless of my circumstance, even mourning, to be a partaker of and conduit for His love, the living waters, through my faith in Jesus who I am called to resemble.

> *"Jesus answered and said unto her,*
> *If you knew the gift of God, and*
> *who it is that said to you, Give Me*
> *to drink; you would have asked of*
> *Him, and He would have given you*
> *living water. The woman said unto*
> *Him, Sir, You have nothing to*
> *draw with, and the well is deep:*
> *from where then have You that*
> *living water? Are You greater than*
> *our father Jacob, which gave us the*
> *well, and drank thereof himself,*
> *and his children, and his cattle?*
> *Jesus answered and said unto her,*
> *Whosoever drinks of this water*
> *shall thirst again: but whosoever*
> *drinks of the water that I shall give*
> *him shall never thirst; but the*
> *water that I shall give him shall be*
> *in him a well of water springing up*
> *into everlasting life"* (John 4:10-14).

In times past, I thought of this young man and still prayed for him. But I also wondered if my Lord used the child as a test set before me to observe my love for others and evaluate my response to one who suffered adversity. I even asked myself, "Could it be possible that I encountered an angel?"

> *"Let brotherly love continue. Be not forgetful to entertain strangers: for thereby some have entertained angels unawares. Remember them that are in bonds, as bound with them; and them which suffer adversity, as being yourselves also in the body" (Hebrews 13:1-3).*

I also thought, "What if my chance meeting with the lad served as a witness and heaven watched to see if I could rise above my own affliction and be a testimony of Christ-like conviction to feed or clothe the poor?" All of my interactions in life would be judged, and in the middle of my torment and battle with principalities I asked myself, "Did I keep the commandments of God? Did I keep my ears open to my Savior's voice and keep in tune with the Father's will for my life?"

"When the Son of Man comes in
His glory, and all the holy angels
with Him, then He will sit on the
throne of His glory. All the nations
will be gathered before Him, and
He will separate them one from
another, as a shepherd divides *his*
sheep from the goats. And He will
set the sheep on His right hand, but
the goats on the left. Then the King
will say to those on His right hand,
'Come, you blessed of My Father,
inherit the kingdom prepared for
you from the foundation of the
world: for I was hungry and you
gave Me food; I was thirsty and
you gave Me drink; I was a
stranger and you took Me in; I *was*
naked and you clothed Me; I was
sick and you visited Me; I was in
prison and you came to Me.' Then
the righteous will answer Him,
saying, 'Lord, when did we see You
hungry and feed *You*, or thirsty,
and give *You* drink? When did we
see You a stranger and take *You* in,
or naked and clothe *You*? Or when

did we see You sick, or in prison,
and come to You?' And the King
will answer and say to them,
'Assuredly, I say to you, inasmuch
as you did it to one of the least of
these My brethren, you did it to
Me'" (*Matthew 25:31-40, NKJV*).

In hindsight, I wish I had done more for the young man. It crossed my mind to drive him to one of the plethora of lodgings in the area and pay for a night, but caution overruled that act of kindness. Instead, I drove away and petitioned heaven for him. I can only hope that the Lord answered my continued prayers for the lad and delivered him from his circumstances. If it was a test or an angelic visit, I hope that a well done or acceptable demonstrative response went out for me.

But what I encountered instilled a deepened view of the frailty of mankind. I hated the influence of the enemy in people's lives. I despised the spell that had them shrouded with a veil that separated them from truth. I discerned many lived in darkness rather than light. Some dwelled in shades of gray where they believed they lived "not so sinful" lifestyles. God spoke to me once as I traveled on an expressway towards an area with black clouds overhead and the threat of a horrific storm ahead. But after I arrived to the area, the sky was gray and I said, "Oh, this is not so bad." God responded to my statement and said, "That is how sin is."

I imagined many who succumbed to transgressions and thought once they were in the sin, "Oh, this is not so bad" instead of having the realization of their captivity in gross darkness.

> "Here you, and give ear; be not proud: for the Lord has spoken. Give glory to the Lord your God, before He cause darkness, and before your feet stumble upon the dark mountains, and, while you look for light, He turn it into the shadow of death, *and* make *it* gross darkness. But if you will not hear it, my soul shall weep in secret places for *your* pride; and mine eye shall weep sore, and run down with tears, because the Lord's flock is carried away captive"

As I journeyed through grief and the Lord intensified my love for the brethren, the sorrow that filled my heart because of the absence of my beloved transferred to others in the bondage of sin. Filled with compassion for their souls, I hated their sin and with fear for their salvation desired to demonstrate the love of God and snatch them from the clutches of the adversary that held them bound. As God kept me from falling and I kept my faith throughout my torment, I wanted the same for them to be presented faultless before our Lord.

> *"But, beloved, remember you the words which were spoken before of the apostles of our Lord Jesus Christ; how that they told you there should be mockers in the last time, who should walk after their own ungodly lusts. These be they who separate themselves, sensual, having not the Spirit. But you, beloved, building up yourselves on your most holy faith, praying in the*

Holy Ghost, keep yourselves in the love of God, looking for the mercy of our Lord Jesus Christ unto eternal life. And of some have compassion, making a difference: and others save with fear, pulling *them* out of the fire; hating even the garment spotted by the flesh. Now unto Him that is able to keep you from falling, and to present *you* faultless before the presence of His glory with exceeding joy, To the only wise God our Savior, be glory and majesty, dominion and power, both now and ever. Amen" (Jude 1:17-25).

Chapter 16

Regrets

I examined why I felt sorriness during my lamentation. I unearthed the dross of what I thought were my husband's desires that I had not fulfilled during our marriage. I skimmed it off and destroyed this mindset so gold would come forth. I realized that regret held me captive and subsequent guilt had me bound.

I learned that separation from my husband gave me a glimpse of what I looked forward to: Being one with Father, Son, and Holy Spirit and joined with thousands upon thousands, which would be so much better than the oneness I had felt with my beloved (John 17:20-23; 1 John 5:7; Daniel 7:9-10). It caused me to regret those times in my marriage where my behavior did not exemplify oneness with my husband and I had operated outside the parameters of unconditional love. Though I was not perfect all the time (for I am in that perfection process), when I reminisced,

I recalled how Ron loved me unconditionally just as I loved him. Absolute love was the specialty and anchor of our marriage that resolved all conflicts as we moved back into oneness with one another.

In comparison, I saw how if I moved myself from being one with my Lord, God the Father, and His Spirit, I existed outside of His love, mercy, and grace to do my own will rather than abide in His. But I also understood the simplicity and ease of returning to the Lord, being one with Him, and lining up with the Word of God—Jesus—in every aspect of my life (Revelation 19:13). I was determined to love God and obey His commandments (1 John 5:1-3). I knew that God desired marriages on earth to mirror our final perfect marriage to the Lamb of God, His Son, and demonstrate His will on earth as in heaven (Revelation 19:7; Matthew 6:10). That may be; however, with remorse, I contemplated how I missed that mark.

I discovered that regret embodied another dimension of bereavement. Mourning included not just sorrow, the sense of loss, and longing for my husband's presence but also brought agony as wrongdoings in my behavior were brought to my consciousness. Contrition expressed remorsefulness that drilled down to guilt that further spiraled to shame. Disdain over my past behavior and attitude toward my beloved glued me to grief. Although I repented of past misdeeds and had asked my husband to forgive me before he departed, memories trapped me as I lamented. Anguish and shame clung to me as I entertained thoughts of how I could have been a better wife.

As I experienced discomfort, part of my pain was thoughts of my own imperfections. I felt as if I wanted to crawl into a hole and not come out as I reflected upon moments where demonstrative love by me did not abound or I had wavered in obedience to the Word of God. I cried a woe unto God as I perceived the condition of my soul and said, "I am undone." Unsettled by my cry, I researched the word "woe" in the Bible and found it was used 106 times from Numbers to Revelation in 98 verses. It gave me pause as I read in Revelation:

"And I beheld, and heard an angel

*flying through the midst of heaven,
saying with a loud voice, Woe,
woe, woe, to the inhabiters of the
earth by reason of the other voices
of the trumpet of the three angels,
which are yet to sound"
(Revelation 8:13)!*

"My God," I said, "three woes at the same time." Nevertheless, in Old Testament Hebrew[16] or New Testament Greek,[17] the word meant the same; "woe" meant alas and/or was an exclamation of grief or lamentation. I recognized my state as being a woman of unclean lips and cried out in dismay. I had a relationship with the Lord, faith in Him, and knew He abided in me and I in Him; yet, I still had not obtained perfection and at times

---

[16] *Word Study Series: The Complete Word Study Old Testament,* General Editor, Warren Baker, D.R.E., *A Concise Dictionary of the Words in the Hebrew Bible; With Their Renderings in the Authorized English Version* by James Strong, S.T.D., LL.D., #188.

[17] *Word Study Series: The Complete Word Study New Testament,* Executive Editor, Spiros Zodhiates, Th.D., *A Concise Dictionary of the Words in The Greek Testament; With Their Renderings in the Authorized English Version* by James Strong, S.T.D., LL.D., #3759.

walked in disobedience. Thrown into disturbance, I considered moments I could have done better. Be that it may, I could not undo that which I regretted and that filled me with sorrow.

I also had to face the fact that I had no partner to share in-home responsibilities. I became flabbergasted at the number of crumbs I dropped. I became disappointed in myself as I recalled my lack of appreciation of chores completed by Ron because I desired him to do more. Now I had to take out the garbage, sit the cans on the curb, and bring them back in. I became aware of what I left behind that had to be cleaned up. As I took on the responsibility of more tasks, I appreciated the tasks that were his and concluded that he had done enough.

I found out that a friend of my husband had died in August of the previous year. From time to time during grief, I thought of him and started to call. I hesitated at first because after my husband departed he had initiated a romanticized pursuit in which I had no interest nor could if I desired. We parted with him leaving the ball in my court to call him.

Because he was a college professor and prolific writer, I wanted to tell him of my book and ask if he would review the manuscript. I felt guilty and saddened at the departure of a dear friend of my husband. He came in town once or twice a year, and my beloved and I always met him for dinner. I felt like a tag-along, but they both wanted me to join them. We enjoyed one another's company with our lively conversations. His death reminded me of things gone, not appreciated while present, and missed.

My reluctance in this fellowship came forth in my spirit as another feeling of disappointment in myself that I had to lay at the feet of Jesus. Satan took every opportunity to keep me in bondage to mourning, and I opened the door to his treachery when I focused on his lies rather than God's truth concerning my past wrongdoings with my husband and in this case reluctance in appreciation of friendship. Hence, I experienced regret that spiraled to guilt and shame.

However, though God caused my grief (Lamentations 3:31-32), the Holy Spirit reminded me that the Lord did not lay accusation upon me. He viewed mourning and His role in the process as a perfecter. Part of my perfection process was to bring to remembrance how through my Savior Jesus the Christ I already overcame regret, guilt, and shame. Jesus strengthened me to walk in that truth and annihilate the enemy's attempt to obliterate my faith and trust in God to give deliverance from that which kept me bound.

When Isaiah cried "woe," the Lord sent a seraph with a live coal to touch his lips and proclaimed his iniquity taken away and his sin purged (Isaiah 6:6-7). With me, the Holy Spirit reminded me of the victory of the cross with the shed blood of Jesus Christ. The pain I experienced with wistfulness Christ had suffered for me and triumphed over it.

> *"God, who at various times and in various ways spoke in time past to the fathers by the prophets, has in these last days spoken to us by His Son, whom He has appointed heir of all things, through whom also He made the worlds; who being the brightness of His glory and the*

express image of His person, and
upholding all things by the word of
His power, when He had by
Himself purged our sins, sat down
at the right hand of the Majesty on
high, having become so much better
than the angels, as He has by
inheritance obtained a more
excellent name than they"
(Hebrews 1:1-4, NKJV).

Shrouded by a veil of mourning, I allowed the devil to torment me with accusations. I listened and did not state, "I am not Eve," nor did I identify the source of lies that rummaged through my mind. Satan's characteristic of slyness enabled him to cloud my thoughts with deception like he did Eve (Genesis 3:1-13) and that deception clothed me with the spirit of regret. I mulled over what the enemy presented. I heeded the wrong voice and succumbed to the taunting of satan that caused me to shift the view of myself from God's perspective to his. The enemy tried to use guilt and shame to negate the work of the cross in my life, steal my peace, make a mockery of the Word of God, and assimilate me into the kingdom of darkness. But the Lord's faithfulness reminded me by His Spirit to be strong, put on His armor—the promises of God—and stand in His truth.

Chapter 17

Tried by Fire

Refined into Gold

*"But who can endure the day of
His coming? And who can stand
when He appears? For He is like a
refiner's fire and like launderers'
soap. He will sit as a refiner and a
purifier of silver; He will purify
the sons of Levi, and purge them as
gold and silver, that they may offer
to the Lord an offering in
righteousness"*
(Malachi 3:2-3, NKJV).

I am called to be a royal priesthood, chosen
to be holy and peculiar unto the Lord (1
Peter 2:9-10). With that in mind, as I
travailed through lamentation the Lord
used it to continue my refinement into a
purified vessel. I learned to focus on God's
perspective and what He wanted to
accomplish in me—that is holiness and

purity. My life though full of grief, I had to push forward and through the pain. The Lord proved, tested, and worked to separate me from those things that lacked perfection and hindered me from being like gold but also prepared me to be much more precious than gold. As part of His character, God positioned me to prove whether or not I would walk in His ways. I ran to Jesus—my only way of escape for the mourning I experienced. I forced my mind to think on Him and what He accomplished on the cross for me.

I shifted my focus from, "God deliver me from this anguish," to the question, "What needed to be changed in me to become like Christ?" I looked at my grief journey as a stay in the wilderness for an assigned time until what needed to die in me did so. Wilderness produced refinement that steered me towards productivity in my calling and resemblance of Jesus. I thought of the Israelites who wandered for 40 years in the wilderness until those who gathered against God died (Numbers 14:32-35).

I also saw the wilderness as a place of refreshment that gave me the strength to continue on. I remembered Elijah who had fled into the wilderness because Jezebel threatened his life; it was where, in despair, he pleaded for God to let him die. But instead the Lord nourished him, spoke with him, and commissioned him with another assignment. His ordeal is told in 1 Kings 19.

I also came to see the wilderness as a place of waiting until the promises of God for my life are fulfilled. I considered David who avoided Saul and fled from wilderness to wilderness until Saul, who sought David's life, died himself and David assumed his destiny as king. His time of anointing, trouble, and the subsequent beginning of appointment as king is described in 1 Samuel 16:1 to 2 Samuel 2:4.

It also occurred to me that the wilderness provided a training atmosphere for the race set before me to become a vessel as ordained from the foundations of the world to be used for the Lord's purpose. I compared mourning to the behavioral and performance change required by me for weight loss, muscle gain, lowered cholesterol, and removal of prediabetes. All involved sacrifice, setbacks, and (in the case of exercise) sometimes pain. I attained accomplishment of goals by not giving up or in to defeat. Practice made the task easier in the next round. I picked myself up and hit restart. I forced myself to apply those same principles to deliverance from grief, with the exception that Christ served as the anchor to discipline and not self. My tenacity was based on the finished work of the cross and surrender to what Jesus desired to change in me and grow me into.

> *"Do you not know that those who run in a race all run, but one receives the prize? Run in such a way that you may obtain it. And everyone who competes for the prize is temperate in all things. Now they do it to obtain a perishable crown, but we for an imperishable crown. Therefore I run thus: not with uncertainty. Thus I fight: not as one who beats the air. But I discipline my body and bring it into subjection, lest, when I have preached to others, I myself should become disqualified"*
> (1 Corinthians 9:24-27, NKJV).

And, last but not least, I realized that the wilderness represented a place of being tested to see if I would stand in the truths of God. I said to myself, "Even Jesus had a wilderness occurrence; and if He did, how much more would I?" The Spirit of God led Jesus into the wilderness to be tempted by the devil that appeared to Him after He had fasted 40 days and 40 nights (Matthew 4:1-3). I surmised that the Word of God defined me, not trials. I understood that my mind, body, soul, and spirit must align with the Word of God. Conviction, repentance, and choice summarized my journey through bereavement that felt like it flung me into a wilderness.

I acknowledged the work of God in my life as I activated my faith, allowed God to refresh me as I languished, waited with patience for God to orchestrate movement towards my destiny, resisted the devil's attempt to take my life in the wilderness, and forced myself to discipline my mind to focus on the accomplished work of the cross and not the sorrow that consumed my life. I decided to continue to build my life upon God's foundation of truth and not the devil's satire of torment. I concluded that God's character insisted that His people endure and be proved by a wilderness season that would result in movement towards purification, holiness, and endowed power to fulfill His purpose—in my case, the next phase He designed for my existence.

> *"Now if any man build upon this*
> *foundation gold, silver, precious*
> *stones, wood, hay, stubble; every*
> *man's work shall be made manifest:*
> *for the day shall declare it, because*
> *it shall be revealed by fire; and the*
> *fire shall try every man's work of*
> *what sort it is"*
> *(1 Corinthians 3:12-13).*

I compared my refinement process to homemade soup or stock preparation. After I have brought my meat and/or vegetables in water to a low boil, foam appears that is skimmed off and discarded. After the contents is cooked, the meat and/or vegetables are removed and the broth is poured through cheesecloth (if not on hand, a coffee filter or even a paper towel) to clarify the liquid. I have also placed unfiltered stock in the refrigerator or freezer, waited until the fat is hardened on the surface, and then removed it. However, before this broth is used in a recipe, I heated and filtered it to remove seasonings that accumulated at the bottom of the pot and any fat that remained to ensure a clear broth, free from unwanted particles.

I compared stock purification to silver refinement whereas impurities called dross float to the top and are poured off. When I looked at gold, one purification process causes impurities to separate on the surface and in another method impurities pass to the bottom as insoluble slime.[18] Both the surface and slime impurities are removed to establish an almost 100% pure gold. Encouraged by the confidence in my Lord's love for me and desire that I become as He intended, in contrast I knew that my refinement process by the Lord once completed would accomplish my not almost but 100% perfection. My journey

---

[18] From Britannica.com, "Gold Processing Refining," https://www.britannica.com/technology/gold-processing/Refining.

through mourning moved that process along as God brought me through the fiery affliction I underwent caused by the departure of my beloved.

> "Behold, I have refined you, but not
> with silver; I have chosen you in
> the furnace of affliction"
> (Isaiah 48:10).

Just as foam and impediments to clarified stock, dross from silver, and impurities and slime from gold are removed to produce clear stock and the purest form of silver and gold, my imperfections had to be removed. The foam, dross, and slime of heaviness and anguish upon me had to be skimmed off, poured out, and discarded to provide God a surrendered vessel ready for His purpose and fulfillment of my destiny.

> "And it shall come to pass, *that* in
> all the land, says the Lord, two
> parts therein shall be cut off *and*
> die; but the third shall be left
> therein. And I will bring the third
> part through the fire, and will

refine them as silver is refined, and
will try them as gold is tried: they
shall call on My name, and I will
hear them: I will say, It *is* My
people: and they shall say, The
Lord *is* my God"
(Zechariah 13:8-9).

God gave me a poem three and one-
half years after the departure of my beloved:

Spring forth, my children, spring forth.
Leave the ashes behind.
(I have burned your desires and flesh.)
Hear my Spirit.
Come my way.
Purity of mind.
Righteousness of spirit.
Holiness of body.
You know the way to the bridal chamber to be
one with me.
Now is the time for the union.
Come.
Enter into my loving bosom.
Enter into my light.
You are my desire and I am yours.
Clothed in white.
Free in flight.

191

During my lamentation, the Holy Spirit spoke to me as I rested one afternoon and said, "God is setting up His kingdom." I asked myself, "Do I measure up to be considered a worthy vessel for His use?"

God's Spirit reminded me of Jehoshaphat's reign where he followed in his father Asa's footsteps and did what was right in the sight of the Lord, except he did not take down the high places because of the people's heart of disobedience (2 Chronicles 20:31-33). I was directed by the Spirit to examine the term "high places." In Hebrew, the word is *bāmâ (bam-maw')* and has the meaning of a stronghold or a high place which was destined for unauthorized worship.[19]

The question to me then became, "What have I erected in my life that is built up higher than God?" Guided by the Spirit of God, with trepidation, I further asked myself, "What waves had I allowed to wash over me that supplanted the rain

[19] *Word Study Series: The Complete Word Study Testament,* General Editor, Warren Baker, D.R.E., Lexical Aids to the Old Testament, #1116.

of the Holy Spirit? What strongholds were activated in my life where I conducted unauthorized worship, ate sacrificial meals, prayed contrary to the will of God, prostituted myself, or sacrificed my children?" I speculated and asked myself, "What value had I placed on those things that usurped, undermined, diminished, or exalted itself over the truths of God or placed above my Lord whether time, money, selfish acts, pride, fornication, idolatry, immorality, revelry, rebellion, unbelief, lawlessness, . . . on and on?" Not that I found myself guilty of all trespasses listed, however, I still measured my behavior and response to my circumstance of grief against them.

In retrospect, as I recalled this analysis of myself in my third year of mourning where I still incurred tribulation, I looked at myself from a different viewpoint and sensed a vessel in a fiery furnace being purified first into silver and then gold. All that I experienced through lamentation, fell prey to, and was held captive by epitomized spirits that exalted themselves over the truth and promises of God with the purpose to steal, kill, and destroy me.

But God accomplished His intent to bring me through the blazed trial of bereavement, cemented me in my faith, exposed and rid me of anything in me that contradicted His Word, and brought me forth as pure gold. He knew and trusted my heart that I knew He would not abandon me in the wilderness of affliction but would strengthen and protect me as I endured my trial and advanced in His kingdom.

"Yes," I said, as God told me in my third year of grief that He is setting up His kingdom; and yes, I can look with assurance that I am part of that kingdom, a new vessel birthed out of fire through the wilderness journey.

> *"Behold, I go forward, but He is not there; and backward, but I cannot perceive Him: on the left hand, where He does work, but I cannot behold Him: He hides Himself on the right hand, that I cannot see Him: But He knows the way that I take: when He has tried me, I shall come forth as gold"*
> *(Job 23:8-10).*

Chapter 18

Epilogue

Victorious Ending

The first week after my beloved's physical death, I heard the Holy Spirit whisper, "No excuse now!" It was a two-fold message the Holy Spirit gave me as a reminder of my purpose on the earth. As a friend of Jesus, He chose and ordained me to do the work prepared beforehand for me to do (John 15:14-16) and for me to, with tenacity, acknowledge my position as His royal priesthood, chosen and called out of darkness into His light (1 Peter 2:9-10). The Spirit of God gave a forewarning of the journey set before me to move forward and accomplish the Father's will for my life and be a testimony of faith and a living sacrifice unto God on the earth. In spite of the torment I endured as I lamented the departure of my husband, God's Spirit renewed my mind and enabled me to overcome grief.

"I beseech you therefore, brethren, by the mercies of God, that you present your bodies a living sacrifice, holy, acceptable unto God, which is your reasonable service. And be not conformed to this world: but be you transformed by the renewing of your mind, that you may prove what is that good, and acceptable, and perfect will of God" (Romans 12:1-2).

To myself, I asked, "How do I cope with death?" I concluded, "Look to life." I became like my precious grandson. As he slept, I looked upon him and saw peace, a sense of safety, no stress, tranquility, and blossoming life. From that aspect, I purposed to tap into the power that radiated from my grandson as he rested. I knew that the embodiment of love from God surrounded him; and that same love resided in me, and I abided in it. I recognized that just as my grandson personified the Lord's heritage—God's reward—so did I (Psalm 127:3).

When I remembered to position myself as a child of God, depend on His peace, enter into His rest, and boldly come to my Daddy for help, I obtained victory over grief (Exodus 14:14; Numbers 6:22-26; Hebrews 4:9-11, 16). I yielded myself to God and restrained emotions that shifted thoughts from the Lord. I acknowledged his authority, responsibility, care, and dominion over me. I tapped into the victory of the cross and allowed the healing virtue of Jesus to flow from Him to me. I decided that my Lord's healing ran like a faucet that He never turned off. I stopped the flow as I permitted grief to cling to me like flypaper.

The trial of grief tried to place a barrier between me and God, but faith kept Him ever before me. I heard the Spirit of God speak, "Have better faith, fight better, stand better, believe better, trust better; then things will get better."

I reached a turning point. One day, I walked through my living room, passed by my beloved's piano, and could not cry. After I experienced the 4th anniversary of Ron's departure, I felt a new release, a breath of fresh air, and a shift in my life. I realized the manifestation of the truth of the cross. The death, burial, and resurrected life of Jesus struck down grief so that I could walk in newness of life (Isaiah 53:4; Romans 6:4).

With gladness I looked back and said, "I lived; and now a different course is set before me, a new beginning—life after death." I survived God's plan for my life, what He wanted me to experience. I learned what the Father desired I become as He gave me room to grow, taught me new depths of faith through His Spirit, and brought to remembrance truths of His Word (John 14:26).

I came to understand that Jesus, my Brother, not only wept for me in the garden but also over me just as He did with Lazarus (Matthew 12:50; Hebrews 5:7-10; John 11:34-44). My Savior, the finisher of faith loosed the graveclothes of death as I bewailed the separation from my husband and brought me into His light and the glory of God. My husband in rightness had adorned me with the title "designated survivor." His journey over mine continued on as I overcame the disruption his death on earth initiated.

My Lord did not fill me with bitterness but instead with His view of perfect love that abided in me and what He destined me to become. I kept in my heart the faithfulness of God and the power of the Holy Spirit. My faith did not fail as I stood in appropriation of His truth and, thereby, assurance materialized that through the mercies of God I would not be consumed by grief.

> "This I recall to my mind,
> Therefore I have hope. Through the
> Lord's mercies we are not
> consumed. Because His
> compassions fail not They are new
> every morning; Great is Your
> faithfulness"
> (Lamentations 3:21-23, NKJV).

The details of my eternal life, though pondered, are unknown to me—with the exception that I will be created to worship Him that made heaven and earth. In conclusion, my destiny fulfilled and the prize obtained. Anything else was just what I had to go through as God perfected me.

I am surprised that I am content with myself as I have accepted who I am and who God designed me to be. After I looked at my life, I saw the thread of my identity from beginning to end from God's eye view and not mine.

Years of visions, dreams, and devotions seemed to unravel before me as I listened to His Spirit remind me of assignments given. I waited and now know it is my time to pursue them for mourning is out of the way. My grief journey came to a close, and only a slight fragrance lingered as a faint hint of perfume from a just opened bottle. Be that as it may, I do recognize that only the Lord can bring about my future. As Moses said, I will not go without His presence. I am not worried; I am not concerned. I am content and waiting.

> *"Now therefore, I pray Thee, if I have found grace in Your sight, show me now Your way, that I may know You, that I may find grace in Your sight: and consider that this nation is Your people. And He said, My Presence shall go with you, and I will give you rest. And*

he said unto Him, If Your Presence
go not with me, carry us not up
hence" (Exodus 33:13-15).

As I came through the fog of grief, the Lord beckoned for me to clothe myself again with an attribute of Christ, "Greater love has no man than this, that a man lay down his life for his friends" (John 15:13). During my bereavement season, I had a dream whereas I conversed with a lighthearted Christ and talked to Him as I would a regular person. He had good things to say about me and told me that wherever I go I would meet opposition if I was going to do His work. We talked as if friends or brother and sister. He called me "friend."

"You are My friends, if you do
whatsoever I command you.
Henceforth I call you not servants;
for the servant knows not what his
lord does: but I have called you
friends; for all things that I have
heard of My Father I have made
known unto you. You have not
chosen Me, but I have chosen you.
. . that you should go and bring

forth fruit, and that your fruit
should remain: that whatsoever you
shall ask of the Father in My
Name, He may give it you"
(John 15:14-16).

Before the Lord departed, I held His feet and expressed a desire to take some of His burden/pain, but then concluded I could not because He took it all already for me. He already bore the cross. But I sensed His command of love for mankind. He took all pain and suffering; now, I through love tell others of this love of God.

"These things I command you, that
you love one another"
(John 15:17).

I determined that my widowhood walk would be a testimony of faith for all to see. I imagined that all of heaven looked upon me as they waited for my manifestation as a son of God who overcame mourning, strengthened what remained in me, and fought to not let it die or be stolen. I was being clothed in white garments with my name written in the Book of Life and confessed by Christ before the Father and all His angels (Revelation 3:2-5). I prayed, "In Jesus' name, Lord, stir up my spirit to do Your work in Your church" (Haggai 1:14-15) and "Help me to be strong and courageous" (Joshua 1:9). I determined that out of my belly would come living waters, and I would labor for the Lord to bring forth His harvest (John 7:38).

Bereavement, as with any of life's trials, set a choice before me. I could choose how I would endure my anguish: Faith-filled or faithless. I chose faith-filled. I rose above, got through, left behind, and rid myself of the spirit of heaviness, pain, loneliness, forlornness, physical tiredness, physical weakness, and whatever feelings or thoughts that took my joy, peace, love, contentment, security, or created lack of movement towards destiny. I removed anything that was not in alignment with the victory of the cross.

In past times, I had experienced battling demons and principalities, even the devil. But this time, I warred against me. I struggled with my emotions, my feelings, my thoughts—even the very air I breathed—until I realized that I had entangled

203

myself in self-pity. The garments of grief I wore were heavy, and I wanted to be free of them, cleansed, and basking in the presence of the Lord. I looked for my spiritual and physical victory. At the same time, I could hear the enemy laughing and saying, "Where is your God now?"

> "My tears have been my meat day
> and night, while they continually
> say unto me, Where is your God?"
> (Psalm 42:3).

God helped me to see and remove every ounce of circumstantial mindset of outcome. He enabled me to be delivered from anguish. In hindsight, I thought lamentation hindered pursuit of ministry after the departure of my husband; but what I came to understand was that bereavement obstructed my ability to see and find myself in the Lord. I had to visualize myself as one with Christ and the Holy Spirit in the Father. Comfort, peace, and joy eluded me because I lost sight of who dwelled in me and who I abided in. I reminded myself of my position and breathed abundant life instead of the pain of grief.

Jesus, my light within me upheld me when mourning sucked the very breath out of me. I attained relief and overcame as I bowed down, worshipped, and cried out to Him from the depths of my soul. My Savior lifted me up as I applied His shed blood to my suffering and His glory was revealed in me to bring me to a place of being like Him, an heir of God.

"And as Moses lifted up the serpent in the wilderness, even so must the Son of Man be lifted up: that whosoever believes in Him should not perish, but have eternal life. For God so loved the world, that He gave His only begotten Son, that whosoever believes in Him should not perish, but have everlasting life" (John 3:14-16).

The enemy wanted me to perish with lamentation and not live through it with faith. He tried to influence me with the spirits of depression, anguish, and anxiety to snuff out my life. He wanted to torment me to my demise. However, he never knew the full picture. He did not know what I thought or where I stood in my faith as I experienced longing for my husband and the life we had. He just hoped for the best and threw his arsenal at me. But I remembered and reconciled to myself that God allowed trials to strengthen me in my faith and put that enemy under my feet.

> "You shall tread upon the lion and adder: the young lion and the dragon shall you trample under feet" (Psalm 91:13).

The Lord reminded me of all that He had taught in preparation for the journey. What He allowed me to experience, from childhood to my current season in life, enabled me to have victory over mourning as I fought for and maintained the promises of God and the accomplishment of the cross in my life—lesson upon lesson, precept upon precept. My Lord prepared me to work out my faith and salvation with fear and trembling (Philippians 2:12). The word "fear" used in this verse means to run away from that which is dread or a terror to you with reverence for and towards God.[20]

Though my Lord caused grief, He did not use it as a battering ram to break down my faith but through my pain encouraged me to hang on to hope for deliverance from anguish. Although a spirit of heaviness sat upon me like a heavy chain, it did not hedge me in as God pointed to the way out: His Son, my Savior and the work of the cross. When I cried and shouted out to the Lord, He did not close His eyes or ears to my prayers but heard me and gave me the desires of my petitions: His will for my life and deliverance from torment of the departure of my beloved.

From the onset, I knew that no sin in my life caused the disruption that led to mourning. I recognized it as a trial my loving Father set before me just as He set the cross before His Son, Christ. At first, I

---

[20] *Word Study Series: The Complete Word Study New Testament,* Spiros Zodhiates, TH.D., Lexical Aids to the New Testament, #5401. The Greek word used here for "fear" is *phóbos* and the explanation is inferred by the verb format *phobéomai.*

said, "If Jesus bore the cross, I could bear grief." But then I came to the conclusion that I did not have to because He took my anguish over the departure of my husband to the cross also. God solidified the absolute truth of the cross through deprivation of my beloved. There is victory over all things for all who believe in Christ. Jesus bore and triumphed over torment for me so that I could become one of His brethren, predestined to be just like Him.

I had to choose not to stand alone in my journey. I encouraged myself in the Lord and kept thrusting myself into His presence over and over again. I did not give up but continued to ask, prayed with incessancy, and wept with perpetuation before the Lord until I obtained release from pain and aloneness. I faced my tribulation and pressed forward toward the mark of who God predestined me to be.

What the cross accomplished came to pass. My faithful Lord raised me up out of anguish. His Spirit daily steered me to search my heart for iniquity and unbelief. I withstood the devil's ploys to exhaust me unto death, and I forced myself into a position and mindset where Christ would find faith in me in spite of the anguish I experienced. I listened to the voice of the Comforter who reminded me of what Jesus said and not to the voice of my adversary who desired my demise. I chose to seek after, follow, and trust the One who died so that I could live and not the one who wanted me to die an eternal death with unbelief.

> *"To him the porter opens; and the sheep hear His voice: and He calls His own sheep by name, and leads them out. And when He puts forth His own sheep, He goes before them, and the sheep follow Him: for they know His voice. And a stranger will they not follow, but will flee from him: for they know not the voice of strangers"*
> *(John 10:3-5).*

I never questioned why Jesus did not heal my husband but accepted the will of God. I acknowledged that sometimes the Lord heals flesh on earth, and sometimes He does not. I believed that God gave bread as healing to His children, and even others were recipients of His miraculous "restore to health" power (Mark 7:25-30). I heard testimonies of the Lord's miraculous healings. I also witnessed those whom He chose not to heal. I knew that there were examples of both in the Bible.

I did what the Lord commanded. I prayed for my husband and believed that through my prayers of faith Jesus would not only forgive his sins and save him but also raise him up from his bed of illness to a healed body (James 5: 14-15). I understood that some waited and expected death when it was pronounced by man. They spoke what man proclaimed. I had the mindset that the medical profession practiced what they received from the Lord, which includes wisdom, skill, knowledge, and understanding to cure the body. But whereas man's expertise had limitations, Jesus had none. I had hoped to see Ron healed on earth; but when that did not occur, my confidence remained that he attained an eternal residence with my Lord Jesus Christ that included the absolute absence of sickness and his spirit free from the bondage of enervated flesh (Revelation

22:1-5). I just had to wrap my mind around, succumb to, and embrace the reality of eternity, a future yet to behold.

I did not question God. I believed in His perfect will for my beloved and understood that my will could not usurp my husband's for perhaps Ron did not want to remain on the earth. The Lord may have honored Ron's will and not my request. Nevertheless, the battle that I faced and obtained victory over drilled down to my ability to let go of what no longer belonged to me.

To my enemy's chagrin, though he tormented me and I suffered through various spirits placed upon me, I stood on "victory is mine" and knew that the demise he desired for me is due for him.

> *"And they went up on the breadth of the earth, and compassed the camp of the saints about, and the beloved city: and fire came down from God out of heaven, and devoured them. And the devil that deceived them was cast into the lake of fire and brimstone, where the beast and the false prophet are,*

and shall be tormented day and
night for ever and ever"
(Revelation 20:9-10).

I have heard people state how long mourning should last. Some good folks said that mourning should take a year, then you should be over it. The Holy Spirit whispered to me, "Two years." It took me four years to stop crying. I concluded that bereavement lasts as long as it takes you to hear, understand, do, or become what the Lord speaks; and what He says moves you closer to being a manifested son of God.

Death awakened many feelings. I experienced its absoluteness but also the majesty of hope that filled me with comfort, peace, and joy. It represented a circumstance that I overcame and moved through to life. The Lord used the departure of my husband as a pruning knife to enable me to bring forth much fruit: His will for my life on earth (John 15:5).

I realized grief had held me as gravity did my feet to the earth. My dreams and hopes had me bound, but I opened a window to my heart and let fresh air in. I allowed the Spirit of God to carry me away toward a new adventure in life and defied the weight of my past life that hung like a millstone around my neck.

Just as the wind blows, I determined that I would go the way of the Lord. I looked in the mirror and asked myself, "Who are you?" I replied, "Go and find out." With my journey through bereavement over, I asked myself, "How am I more like Christ?" and "What characteristics of Christ are enhanced or added to my nature?"

God promised His saints would take and possess His everlasting kingdom for it would be given unto them (Daniel 7:18, 27). I looked forward to my future foretold, and I pushed forth to accomplish my destiny. My eyes beheld a new me as I dispelled grief from my life. My spirit heard my Savior's voice, and I overcame suffering just like Christ. I rejoiced and let my faith overcome mourning.

"Behold, I stand at the door, and knock: if any man hear My voice, and open the door, I will come in to him, and will sup with him, and he

with Me. To him that overcomes
will I grant to sit with Me in My
Throne, even as I also overcame,
and am set down with My Father
in His Throne"
(Revelation 3:20-21).

I exclaimed the first week after my beloved departed, "Oh Jesus, I need you to propel me into Your kingdom purposes!" and "Oh God, do not take Your mercy and grace from me." I proclaimed, "Your blood has washed me!" What I said at the beginning of my journey through grief applies as I rejoice in the victory won and look forward to the next chapter of my life.